**Volume 1** Topics 1–7

## Authors

**Randall I. Charles**
Professor Emeritus
Department of Mathematics
San Jose State University
San Jose, California

**Jennifer Bay-Williams**
Professor of Mathematics
Education
College of Education and Human
Development
University of Louisville
Louisville, Kentucky

**Robert Q. Berry, III**
Professor of Mathematics
Education
Department of Curriculum,
Instruction and Special Education
University of Virginia
Charlottesville, Virginia

**Janet H. Caldwell**
Professor Emerita
Department of Mathematics
Rowan University
Glassboro, New Jersey

**Zachary Champagne**
Assistant in Research
Florida Center for Research in
Science, Technology, Engineering,
and Mathematics (FCR-STEM)
Jacksonville, Florida

**Juanita Copley**
Professor Emerita
College of Education
University of Houston
Houston, Texas

**Warren Crown**
Professor Emeritus of Mathematics
Education
Graduate School of Education
Rutgers University
New Brunswick, New Jersey

**Francis (Skip) Fennell**
Professor Emeritus of
Education and Graduate and
Professional Studies
McDaniel College
Westminster, Maryland

**Karen Karp**
Professor of
Mathematics Education
School of Education
Johns Hopkins University
Baltimore, Maryland

**Stuart J. Murphy**
Visual Learning Specialist
Boston, Massachusetts

**Jane F. Schielack**
Professor Emerita
Department of Mathematics
Texas A&M University
College Station, Texas

**Jennifer M. Suh**
Associate Professor for
Mathematics Education
George Mason University
Fairfax, Virginia

**Jonathan A. Wray**
Mathematics Supervisor
Howard County Public Schools
Ellicott City, Maryland

**SAVVAS**
LEARNING COMPANY

ISBN-13: 978-0-13-495370-0
ISBN-10: 0-13-495370-3

16 2022

# Digital Resources

You'll be using these digital resources throughout the year!

## Go to SavvasRealize.com

 **Interactive Student Edition**
Access online or offline.

 **Interactive Additional Practice Workbook**
Access online or offline.

 **Videos**
Watch Math Practices Animations, Another Look Videos, and clips to support 3-Act Math.

 **Math Tools**
Explore math with digital tools.

**A-Z** **Glossary**
Read and listen in English and Spanish.

 **Visual Learning**
Interact with visual learning animations.

 **Activity**
Solve a problem and share your thinking.

 **Practice Buddy**
Do interactive practice online.

 **Games**
Play math games to help you learn.

 **Assessment**
Show what you've learned.

**SAVVAS realize™** Everything you need for math anytime, anywhere

# Contents

**Digital Resources at SavvasRealize.com**

And remember your Interactive Student Edition is available at SavvasRealize.com!

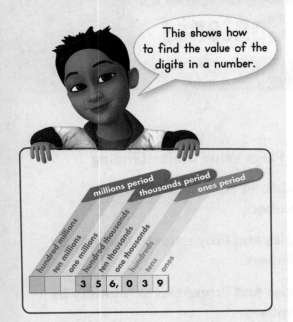

This shows how to find the value of the digits in a number.

millions period
thousands period
ones period

hundred millions
ten millions
one millions
hundred thousands
ten thousands
one thousands
hundreds
tens
ones

3 5 6, 0 3 9

# TOPIC 1 Generalize Place Value Understanding

This shows one way to add whole numbers.

$$\begin{array}{r} \overset{1\ 1}{9{,}263} \\ +\ 7{,}951 \\ \hline 17{,}214 \end{array}$$

# TOPIC 2 Fluently Add and Subtract Multi-Digit Whole Numbers

This shows how to use partial products to multiply.

6 hundreds  12 tens  15 ones

245
×     3
─────
     15
    120  ← Partial products
+  600
─────
    735

# TOPIC 3 Use Strategies and Properties to Multiply by 1-Digit Numbers

This shows how you can represent partial products to help multiply.

$10 \times 10 = 100$

$10 \times 5 = 50$

15

12

$2 \times 10 = 20$

$2 \times 5 = 10$

# TOPIC 4 Use Strategies and Properties to Multiply by 2-Digit Numbers

This shows how place value can help you divide.

# TOPIC 5 Use Strategies and Properties to Divide by 1-Digit Numbers

This shows how you can represent a comparison situation.

42

3 | *n* times as many →

# TOPIC 6 Use Operations with Whole Numbers to Solve Problems

This shows how you can use arrays to model factor pairs for a number.

# TOPIC 7 Factors and Multiples

# TOPIC 8 in volume 2
## Extend Understanding of Fraction Equivalence and Ordering

# TOPIC 9 in volume 2
## Understand Addition and Subtraction of Fractions

## TOPIC 10 in volume 2
## Extend Multiplication Concepts to Fractions

## TOPIC 11 in volume 2
## Represent and Interpret Data on Line Plots

# TOPIC 12 in volume 2
## Understand and Compare Decimals

# TOPIC 13 in volume 2
## Measurement: Find Equivalence in Units of Measure

# TOPIC 14 in volume 2

## Algebra: Generate and Analyze Patterns

# TOPIC 15 in volume 2

## Geometric Measurement: Understand Concepts of Angles and Angle Measurement

# TOPIC 16 in volume 2
## Lines, Angles, and Shapes

# Math Practices and Problem Solving Handbook

The **Math Practices and Problem Solving Handbook** is available at SavvasRealize.com.

**Math Practices**

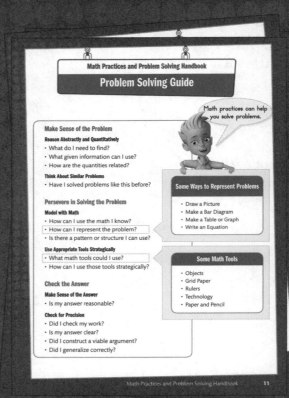

**Problem Solving Guide**
**Problem Solving Recording Sheet**
**Bar Diagrams**

# Generalize Place Value Understanding

**Essential Questions:** How are greater numbers written? How can whole numbers be compared? How are place values related?

**Digital Resources**

Interactive Student Edition | Activity | Visual Learning | Video | Practice

Assessment | Games | Tools | Glossary

Water, wind, and ice can change the shapes of rocks over thousands of years. This is called erosion.

Kannesteinen Rock in Norway got its shape from the sea that surrounds it.

Mountains, caves, and some islands are kinds of rock formations. Here is a project about caves and greater numbers.

## enVision STEM Project: Caves

**Do Research** Use the Internet or other sources to find the depths in feet of the 5 deepest caves in the world.

**Journal: Write a Report** Include what you found. Also in your report:

- Make a place-value chart that includes the five depths.

- Write each depth in expanded form.

- Use "greater than" or "less than" to compare the depths of two of the caves.

Name_____

# Review What You Know

**A-Z Vocabulary**

Choose the best term from the box.
Write it on the blank.

- expanded form
- place value
- number line
- rounding
- number name
- whole numbers

1. The numbers 0, 1, 2, 3, 4, and so on are called _____.

2. A number written using only words is written using a _____.

3. Replacing a number with a number that tells about how many or how much is called _____.

4. _____ is the value given to the place of a digit in a number.

## Comparing Numbers

Compare each set of numbers using >, <, or =.

**5.** 201 ◯ 21

**6.** 313 ◯ 313

**7.** 289 ◯ 290

**8.** 7 ◯ 70

**9.** 725 ◯ 726

**10.** 82 ◯ 82

**11.** 614 ◯ 641

**12.** 618 ◯ 618

**13.** 978 ◯ 987

## Place Value

Tell if the underlined digit is in the ones, tens, hundreds, or thousands place.

**14.** 9,482

**15.** 8,000

**16.** 1,506

**17.** 8,005

**18.** 5,100

**19.** 2,731

In this topic, you will learn more about place value.

## Rounding

**20. Construct Arguments** Use the number line to describe how to round 450 to the nearest hundred.

400        450        500

Name_____

**PROJECT
1A**

## How many bones are in your body?

**Project:** Make a Bones Poster

**PROJECT
1B**

## Would you like to be a construction manager?

**Project:** Design a Building

**PROJECT
1C**

## Which stadium is your favorite?

**Project:** Create a Stadium Model

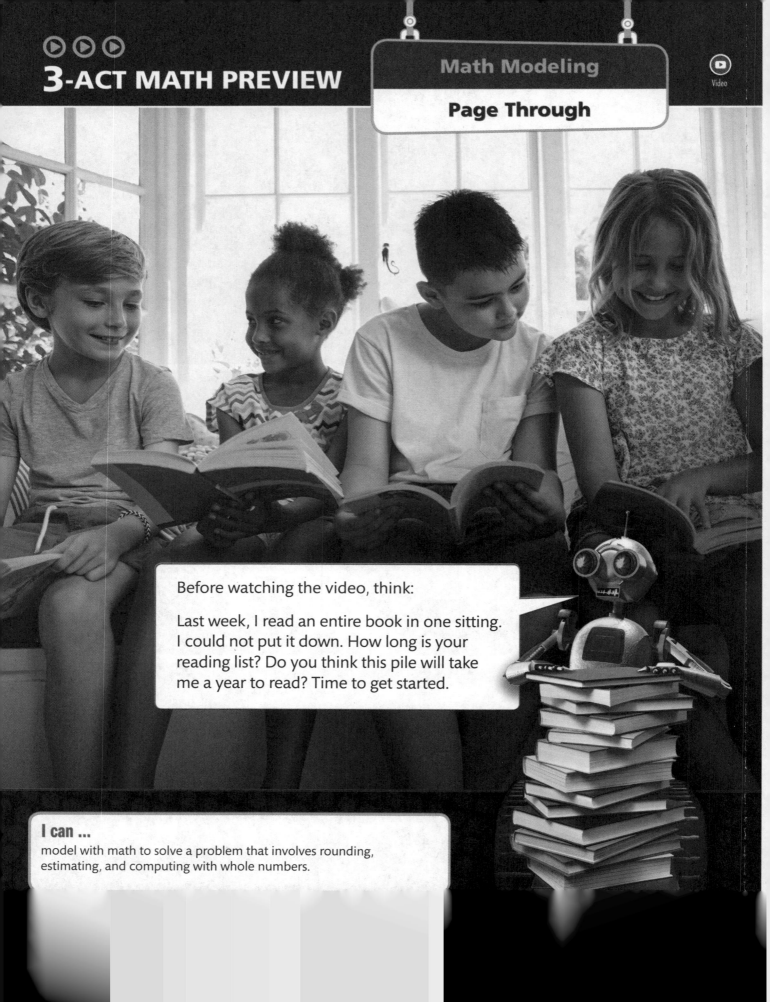

Before watching the video, think:

Last week, I read an entire book in one sitting. I could not put it down. How long is your reading list? Do you think this pile will take me a year to read? Time to get started.

**I can ...**
model with math to solve a problem that involves rounding, estimating, and computing with whole numbers.

Name_____

**Solve & Share**

Mrs. Darcy saved ten $100 bills. How much money did Mrs. Darcy save?

**I can ...**
read and write numbers through one million in expanded form, with numerals, and using number names.

**I can also** reason about math.

You can use reasoning in solving a problem. Think about what you know about ten $10 bills to help you find how much money you would have if you had ten $100 bills.

**Look Back!** How did you decide how many zeros you needed to write in your answer?

**Essential Question**

# What Are Some Ways to Write Numbers to One Million?

**A**

*The graph shows the attendance at a ballpark over one year. Write the total attendance in expanded form and using number names.*

Place value is the position of a digit in a number that tells the value of the digit.

Baseball Attendance

356,039

300,000

200,000

100,000

One Year

**B** The place-value chart shows periods of three places, starting at the ones period from the right and including the thousands and millions period. Each period is separated by a comma and has three place values: ones, tens, and hundreds.

Each digit in 356,039 is written in its place on the chart. Expanded form shows the sum of the values of each digit.

*Expanded form:* 300,000 + 50,000 + 6,000 + 30 + 9

*Number name:* three hundred fifty-six thousand, thirty-nine

millions period · thousands period · ones period

hundred millions · ten millions · one millions · hundred thousands · ten thousands · one thousands · hundreds · tens · ones

| | | | 3 | 5 | 6, | 0 | 3 | 9 |

Notice the comma separates the periods when the number name is written.

**Convince Me!** **Look for Relationships** What pattern exists in the three places in each period?

Name_____

**Solve & Share**

Place-value blocks are shown below for 1, 10, and 100. What patterns in the shapes and sizes of the blocks do you see?

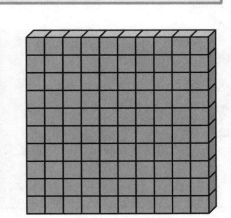

**I can ...**
recognize that a digit in one place has ten times the value of the same digit in the place to its right.

**I can also** generalize from examples.

Use reasoning. You can use place value to analyze the relationship between the digits of a number.

**Look Back!** Describe two ways 100 and 10 are related.

**Essential Question**

# How Are Place Values Related to Each Other?

**A**

Kiana had bottle caps. She wants to collect ten times as many bottle caps. How many bottle caps will Kiana have in her collection then?

Think place value.

100 bottle caps

**B** A hundreds flat represents 100 bottle caps.

100

**C** To find ten times as many bottle caps, group 10 hundreds flats together.

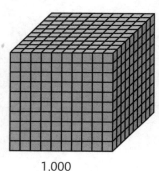

1,000

One thousand is ten times 100.

$100 \times 10 = 1,000$

One hundred is one-tenth of 1,000.

$1,000 \div 10 = 100$

Kiana will have 1,000 bottle caps in her collection.

**Convince Me!** **Generalize** Use place-value blocks to model 1 and 10, 10 and 100, 100 and 1,000. What pattern do you see?

## Another Example!

Joe scored 2,000 points on a progressive video game. It took him 5 weeks to get his total point value to 20,000. It took him 3 months to get his total point value to 200,000 points. How many times greater than his first score were his points after 5 weeks? After 3 months?

After 5 weeks, Joe's points were 10 times greater.

After 3 months, Joe's points were 100 times greater.

$2,000 \times 10 = 20,000$

$20,000 \times 10 = 200,000$

$10 \times 10 = 100$

## ☆ Guided Practice

### Do You Understand?

1. Is the value of the 2 in 23,406 ten times as great as the value of the 3? Explain.

### Do You Know How?

For **2**, use the relationship between the values of the digits to solve.

2. Write a number in which the value of the 3 is ten times greater than the value of the 3 in 135,864.

$3 3 3, 3 3 3$ ✓

## ☆ Independent Practice ☆

For **3–5**, use the relationship between the values of the digits to solve.

3. Baseten School District bought 5,000 pencils. They are distributing the pencils evenly to 10 schools in the district. How many pencils will each school get?

4. Place Elementary School is raising money. They raise $90 a week. How long will it take them to raise $900?

5. A donation of 50 rulers was given to Value Elementary School. The school had 10 times as many erasers donated. How many erasers were donated?

# Problem Solving

**6.** What can you say about the 3s in 43,862 and 75,398?

They are in diffrent Pi ases are afferant and 43,862 is grater than 75,398.

**7. Critique Reasoning** Mia says in 5,555, all the digits have the same value. Is Mia correct? Explain.

Each 5 is worth a difrent vally ew.

**8. Number Sense** In 1934, there was an extreme drought in the Great Plains. In the number 1,934, is the value of the 9 in the hundreds place ten times as great as the value of the 3 in the tens place? Explain.

**9. Critique Reasoning** Vin says in 4,346, one 4 is 10 times as great as the other 4. Is Vin correct? Explain.

**10.** Describe 2 ways to find the area of the shaded rectangle.

 = **1 square unit**

**11. Higher Order Thinking** In 448,244, how is the relationship between the first pair of 4s the same as the relationship between the second pair of 4s?

---

**12.** Which group of numbers shows the values of the 4s in 44,492?

    Ⓐ 40,000; 4,000; 400

    Ⓑ 40,000; 400; 40

    Ⓒ 4,000; 400; 4

    Ⓓ 400; 40; 4

**13.** In which number is the value of the red digit ten times as great as the value of the blue digit?

    Ⓐ **3**35,5**3**1

    Ⓑ 335,**5**31

    Ⓒ 335,5**3**1

    Ⓓ 335,5**3**1

Name _____

## Solve & Share

A robotic submarine can dive to a depth of 26,000 feet. Which oceans can the submarine explore all the way to the bottom? **Solve this problem any way you choose.**

**I can ...**
use place value to compare numbers and record my comparisons using <, =, or >.

**I can also** model with math.

You can model with math. Use what you know about place value to help solve the problem.

| Ocean | Depth |
| --- | --- |
| Atlantic | 28,232 ft |
| Pacific | 35,840 ft |
| Indian | 23,376 ft |

DATA

**Look Back!** Which of the oceans listed is the shallowest? Explain.

**A**

Earth is not perfectly round. The North Pole is 6,356 kilometers from Earth's center. The equator is 6,378 kilometers from the center. Which is closer to Earth's center, the North Pole or the equator?

North Pole: 6,356 km from center

Earth's Center

Equator: 6,378 km from center

The symbol > means "is greater than," and the symbol < means "is less than."

**B** **Step 1**

Write the numbers, lining up places. Begin at the left and compare.

6,356
6,378

The thousands digit is the same in both numbers.

**C** **Step 2**

Look at the next digit. Compare the hundreds.

6,356
6,378

The hundreds digit is also the same in both numbers.

**D** **Step 3**

The first place where the digits are different is the tens place. Compare the tens.

6,356    5 tens < 7 tens,
6,378    so 6,356 < 6,378.

The North Pole is closer than the equator to Earth's center.

**Convince Me!** **Reasoning** Is a whole number with 4 digits always greater than or less than a whole number with 3 digits? Explain.

Name _____

☆ ☆
**Solve & Share**

List 7 numbers that round to 300. Use a variety of numbers. *Solve this problem any way you choose.*

**I can ...**
use place value to round numbers.

**I can also** use a math tool to solve a problem.

Select and use appropriate tools. A number line can help you round numbers.

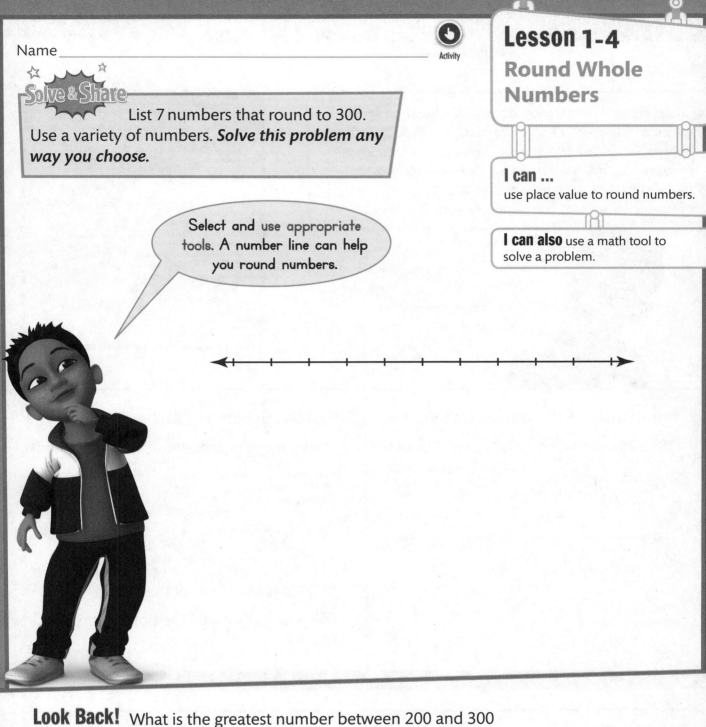

**Look Back!** What is the greatest number between 200 and 300 that is closer to 200 than 300? Explain.

**How Can You Round Numbers?**

**A**

James researched 10 facts about Tallahassee, Florida for an assignment. One of the facts he found was the population in Tallahassee for the year 2017. He chose to round the population on his Florida Facts poster. If James rounded the population in 2017 to the nearest thousand, what was the number James displayed?

When you round, you find which benchmark numbers, or multiples of 10, 100, 1,000, and so on, a number is closest to.

2017 Census
Tallahassee, Florida

TOTAL POPULATION
**181,376**

**B**

Round 181,376 to the nearest thousand.

181,376 is between 181,000 and 182,000.

```
|————————————————|—————→
181,000          182,000
```

**C**

Find the number 181,376 is closer to.

Mark the halfway point on the number line.

If the number is to the left of the halfway point, it rounds down.    If the number is to the right of the halfway point, it rounds up.

```
        181,376
←———|——————|———————|————→
181,000   181,500   182,000
        halfway point
```

181,376 is to the left of the halfway point.

The poster displayed the population as 181,000.

---

**Convince Me!** **Critique Reasoning** Ellie says, "When I round these three numbers, I get the same number for two of them." Anthony says, "Hmmm, when I round these numbers, I get the same number for all three." Who is correct? Explain.

| Three Numbers | | |
|---|---|---|
| 1,483 | 1,250 | 1,454 |

**Another Example!**

You can use place value to round. Round 181,376 to the nearest hundred.

- Find the digit in the rounding place.
- Look at the next digit to the right.
  If it is 5 or greater, add 1 to the rounding digit.
  If it is less than 5, leave the rounding digit alone.
- Change all digits to the right of the rounding place to 0.

181,376
↓↓↓
181,400

Since 7 > 5, the 3 becomes a 4.

# Guided Practice

### Do You Understand?

1. Explain how to round a number when 3 is the digit to the right of the rounding place.

2. What number is halfway between 421,000 and 422,000?

### Do You Know How?

For **3–8**, round each number to the place of the underlined digit.

3. 12<u>8</u>,955

4. 85,6<u>3</u>9

5. <u>9</u>,924

6. 19<u>4</u>,524

7. <u>1</u>60,656

8. <u>1</u>49,590

# Independent Practice

For **9–24**, use a number line or place value to round each number to the place of the underlined digit.

9. 4<u>9</u>3,295

10. <u>3</u>9,230

11. <u>2</u>77,292

12. 54,<u>8</u>46

13. 4,0<u>2</u>8

14. <u>6</u>38,365

15. 453,<u>2</u>80

16. 17,<u>9</u>09

17. <u>9</u>56,000

18. 5<u>5</u>,460

19. 3<u>2</u>1,679

20. 417,5<u>4</u>7

21. 1<u>1</u>7,821

22. <u>7</u>5,254

23. 9<u>4</u>9,999

24. 666,<u>8</u>21

# Problem Solving

**25.** For each zoo in the table, round the attendance to the nearest hundred thousand.

| Zoo Attendance | |
|---|---|
| Zoo D | 234,679 |
| Zoo E | 872,544 |
| Zoo F | 350,952 |

**26. Number Sense** Write four numbers that round to 700,000 when rounded to the nearest hundred thousand.

**27. Reasoning** A forest ranger correctly rounded the number of visitors to a park to be 120,000 visitors. Write a number that could be the actual number of visitors if he rounded to the nearest ten thousand.

**28.** Amy counted the number of boys and girls at a party. She recorded the results in the tally chart below.

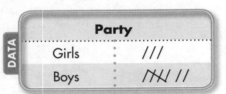

| Party | |
|---|---|
| Girls | /// |
| Boys | /// // |

How many more boys than girls were at the party?

**29. Higher Order Thinking** Liz attended class every day since she started school as a kindergartner. She said she has been in school for about 1,000 days. What numbers could be the actual number of school days if Liz rounded to the nearest ten?

## ✓ Assessment Practice

**30.** Complete the table. Round each number to the given place.

| Number | Ten | Hundred | Thousand | Ten Thousand |
|---|---|---|---|---|
| 45,982 | | | | |
| 128,073 | | | | |
| 13,713 | | | | |
| 60,827 | | | | |
| 105,307 | | | | |

Name_____

**Solve & Share**

The land areas of three states are shown in the table. Mickey said Alaska's land area is about 10 times greater than Georgia's land area. Explain why Mickey is or is not correct. Construct a math argument to support your answer.

| State | Land Area (in square miles) |
|-------|------------------------------|
| Alaska | 570,641 |
| Georgia | 57,513 |
| Hawaii | 6,423 |

**I can ...**
construct arguments using what I know about place-value relationships.

**I can also** compare numbers using place value.

## Thinking Habits
*Be a good thinker! These questions can help you.*

- How can I use numbers, objects, drawings, or actions to justify my argument?

- Am I using numbers and symbols correctly?

- Is my explanation clear and complete?

**Look Back!** **Construct Arguments** Mary said Georgia's land area is about 10 times greater than Hawaii's land area. Is Mary correct? Construct a math argument to support your answer.

**Essential Question**

# How Can You Construct Arguments?

**A**

*The table shows the retail sales per person in three states. Bella says Arizona had more retail sales per person than Massachusetts.*

| State | Retail Sales per Person |
|-------|------------------------|
| Arizona | $13,637 |
| Iowa | $13,172 |
| Massachusetts | $13,533 |

**How can you construct a math argument that supports Bella's conjecture?**

I will use what I know about place value to compare numbers.

*A conjecture is a statement that is believed to be true but has not been proven.*

**B**

**How can I construct an argument?**

**I can**

- give an explanation that is clear and complete.

- use numbers and symbols correctly in my explanation.

- use numbers, objects, drawings, or actions to justify my argument.

- use a counterexample in my argument.

**C**

*Here's my thinking.*

Bella's statement makes sense.

Start with the greatest place value. The digits are the same in the **ten thousands place** and in the **thousands place**. The digits are different in the **hundreds place**, so that place is compared.

$13,6$37
$13,5$33

**600 > 500**

So, $13,637 > $13,533.

Bella is correct. Arizona had more retail sales per person than Massachusetts.

**Convince Me!** **Construct Arguments** Gayle said Arizona had more retail sales than Massachusetts because 7 > 3, so $13,637 > $13,533. Construct an argument to explain whether or not Gayle is correct.

Practice  Tools  Assessment

# ☆Guided Practice

### Construct Arguments

Use the table on the previous page. Jorge said Massachusetts has more retail sales per person than Iowa.

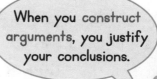

When you construct arguments, you justify your conclusions.

1. What numbers would you use to construct an argument supporting Jorge's conjecture?

2. How could you support Jorge's conjecture?

3. Is Jorge's conjecture true? Justify your answer.

# Independent Practice ☆

### Construct Arguments

The population of Gerald's city is three hundred thousand, twenty-seven. Gerald wrote the number as 327,000. Emily lives in a city that has a population of three hundred sixteen thousand, forty-two. Gerald concluded that his city's population is greater than the population of Emily's city.

4. Does Gerald's explanation make sense? Identify any flaws in Gerald's thinking.

5. Construct a math argument that explains why Gerald did not write the population of his city correctly.

6. Correct Gerald's argument. Explain how to compare the populations of Gerald's and Emily's cities.

# Problem Solving

**Performance Task**

**Planets**

The planets in our solar system are different sizes, as shown below. Nora conjectured that Jupiter's equator is about 10 times as long as Earth's equator.

**Length of Equators for 4 Planets**

Earth 40,030 km    Jupiter 439,264 km    Venus 38,025 km    Mars 21,297 km

7. **Make Sense and Persevere** What information do you have?

8. **Be Precise** What are possible estimates for the lengths of the equators of Jupiter and Earth?

When you construct arguments, you explain clearly and completely.

9. **Reasoning** What is the relationship between the estimates you found for the lengths of the two equators?

10. **Construct Arguments** Construct an argument justifying Nora's conjecture.

Name_____

# Fluency Review Activity

Find a partner. Get paper and pencil. Each partner chooses a different color: Light blue or dark blue.

Partner 1 and Partner 2 each point to a black number at the same time. Both partners multiply those numbers.

If the answer is on your color, you get a tally mark. Work until one partner has twelve tally marks.

**I can ...**
multiply within 100.

**I can also** make math arguments.

**Partner 1**

| 6 |
| 9 |
| 8 |
| 5 |
| 7 |

| 40 | 28 | 45 | 56 |
| 24 | 24 | 36 | 20 |
| 63 | 48 | 63 | 64 |
| 15 | 42 | 49 | 32 |
| 54 | 27 | 35 | 21 |
| 72 | 72 | 18 | 81 |

**Partner 2**

| 7 |
| 4 |
| 3 |
| 9 |
| 8 |

**Tally Marks for Partner 1**

**Tally Marks for Partner 2**

Glossary

**Word List**

- conjecture
- expanded form
- greater than symbol (>)
- less than symbol (<)
- millions
- period
- place value
- rounding

## Understand Vocabulary

Choose the best term from the box. Write it on the blank.

**1.** A group of three digits, separated by commas, starting from the right is called a _____.

**2.** A process that determines which multiple of 10, 100, 1,000 (and so on) a number is closest to is called _____.

**3.** A statement that is believed to be true but has not yet been proven is called a _____.

**4.** The value given to a place a digit has in a number is called its _____.

**5.** In a number, a period of three places to the left of the thousands period is called the _____ period.

For each of these terms, give an example and a non-example.

|  | Example | Non-example |
|---|---|---|
| **6.** greater than symbol (>) | _____ | _____ |
| **7.** less than symbol (<) | _____ | _____ |
| **8.** expanded form | _____ | _____ |

## Use Vocabulary in Writing

**9.** Describe the value of the 9 in 926,415. Use at least 2 terms from the Word List in your explanation.

**Set A** pages 5–8 _____

Use a place-value chart to write 301,400.

**Expanded form:** 300,000 + 1,000 + 400

**Number name:** three hundred one thousand, four hundred

**Remember** that each period has hundreds, tens, ones, and the period name.

Write each number in expanded form and using number names.

**1.** 7,549

**2.** 92,065

**Set B** pages 9–12 _____

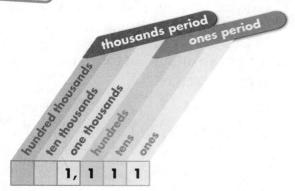

1,111 = 1,000 + 100 + 10 + 1

As you move left, each numeral is 10 times greater than the digit on its right.

$1 \times 10 = 10$
$10 \times 10 = 100$
$100 \times 10 = 1,000$

**Remember** to use the relationship between the values of the digits.

For **1–2**, solve.

**1.** How many times greater is the value of the 7 in 70,048 than the value of 7 in 17,992?

**2.** Violet has 30 glass tiles. She would like to mosaic tile a tabletop with 10 times that number of tiles. How many tiles does Violet want to use?

**Set C** pages 13–16 _____

Use place value to compare 45,423 and 44,897. Start comparing from the left. Look for the first digit that is different.

           **45,423   44,897**

                 **5 > 4**

             5,000 > 4,000

So, 45,423 > 44,897.

**Remember** that you can use place value to compare numbers.

Write < or > in the ◯.

**1.** 291,846 ◯ 291,864

**2.** 662,980 ◯ 66,298

**3.** 88,645 ◯ 87,645

Round 764,802 to the nearest hundred thousand.

764,802

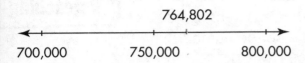

700,000        750,000        800,000

764,802 is to the right of the halfway point. So, 764,802 rounds to 800,000.

**Remember** to find the halfway point to help you round.

For **1–4**, use number lines or place value to round each number to the place of the underlined digit.

1. 166,742

2. 76,532

3. 5,861

4. 432,041

Think about these questions to help you **construct arguments**.

## Thinking Habits

- How can I use numbers, objects, drawings, or actions to justify my argument?

- Am I using numbers and symbols correctly?

- Is my explanation clear and complete?

**Remember** that you can use math to show why your argument is correct.

According to the 2000 census, the population of a city was 935,426. According to the 2010 census, the population of the same city was 934,578. Taylor says the 2000 population was greater than the 2010 population.

1. Construct an argument that supports Taylor's conjecture.

2. In 1870, the population was seventy-two thousand, five hundred six. Lupita wrote 72,560. Construct a math argument that explains whether Lupita wrote the number correctly.

Name_____

## Video Games

Tanji, Arun, and Juanita are playing a video game with 3 levels. The opportunity to earn points increases as the levels of the game increase. To keep track of their progress, Tanji, Arun, and Juanita record and examine their scores at each level.

1. Use the **Level 1** table to answer the following questions.

### Part A

Tanji noticed he was the only player with 3s in his Level 1 score. What are the values of the 3s in Tanji's score?

### Part B

Arun noticed the 5s in his score were next to each other. Describe the relationship between the 5s in Arun's score.

| Level 1 | |
|---|---|
| **Player** | **Score** |
| Tanji | 4,337 |
| Arun | 5,519 |
| Juanita | 2,868 |

DATA

### Part C

Juanita says the value of one 8 in her score is ten times greater than the value of the other 8. Construct an argument and draw a place-value chart to determine if Juanita is correct.

**2.** Use the **Level 2** table to answer the following questions.

| Level 2 | |
| --- | --- |
| **Player** | **Score** |
| Tanji | 56,899 |
| Arun | 39,207 |
| Juanita | 60,114 |

DATA

### Part A

Juanita had the greatest score at Level 2, followed by Tanji and Arun. Write each player's score in expanded form to compare each score by place value.

### Part B

Write each player's score using number names.

### Part C

Use >, =, or < to write comparisons between the Level 2 scores.

### Part D

Arun noticed his Level 2 score has a greater value in the thousands place than Tanji's and Juanita's Level 2 scores. Round Arun's score to the nearest thousand.

# Fluently Add and Subtract Multi-Digit Whole Numbers

**Essential Questions:** How can sums and differences of whole numbers be estimated? What are standard procedures for adding and subtracting whole numbers?

**Digital Resources**

Interactive Student Edition  Activity  Visual Learning  Video  Practice

Assessment  Games  Tools  Glossary

The faster an object is moving, the more energy it has.

In 1970, a rocket-powered vehicle was the first to travel over 1,000 kilometers per hour!

That takes a lot of energy! Here is a project on speed and comparing speeds.

## enVision STEM Project: The World's Fastest Vehicles

**Do Research** Since 1970, the speed record has been broken many times. Use the Internet or other sources to find five vehicles that can go faster than 1,000 kilometers per hour.

**Journal: Write a Report** Include what you found. Also in your report:

- Make a table that includes the type of vehicle, whether the vehicle moves on land, water, or in space, and the speed of the vehicle.

- Use place value to find the fastest and the slowest vehicle in your table.

- Calculate the difference between the speeds of two of the vehicles in your table.

Name _____

# Review What You Know

**A-Z Vocabulary**

Choose the best term from the box.
Write it on the blank.

| | |
|---|---|
| • equation | • period |
| • estimate | • rounding |

1. An _____ is an approximate number or answer.

2. A process that determines which multiple of 10, 100, 1,000, and so on a number is closest to is called _____.

3. A number sentence that uses the equal sign (=) to show two expressions have the same value is an _____.

## Addition Facts and Mental Math

Find each sum.

| | | |
|---|---|---|
| **4.** $4 + 6$ | **5.** $7 + 5$ | **6.** $29 + 8$ |
| **7.** $14 + 5$ | **8.** $13 + 7$ | **9.** $37 + 7$ |
| **10.** $289 + 126$ | **11.** $468 + 329$ | **12.** $157 + 211$ |

## Subtraction Facts and Mental Math

Find each difference.

| | | |
|---|---|---|
| **13.** $27 - 3$ | **14.** $6 - 4$ | **15.** $15 - 8$ |
| **16.** $11 - 8$ | **17.** $66 - 2$ | **18.** $17 - 8$ |
| **19.** $416 - 404$ | **20.** $220 - 205$ | **21.** $148 - 106$ |

## Rounding

22. **Construct Arguments** Why does 843,000 round to 840,000 rather than 850,000 when rounded to the nearest ten thousand?

A good math explanation should be clear, complete, and easy to understand.

Name_____

## PROJECT 2A

**What are the largest cities in your home state?**

**Project:** Map the Population of Your State's Largest Cities

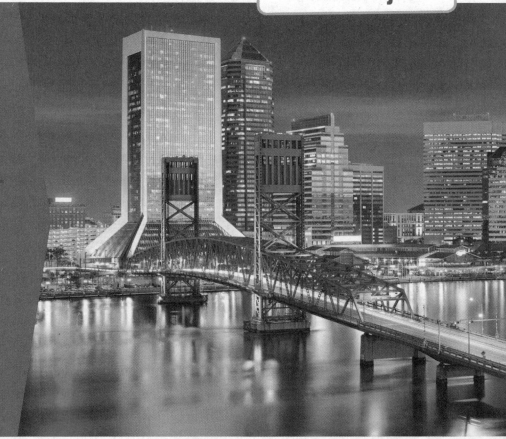

## PROJECT 2B

**How did the United States become a nation?**

**Project:** Write a Report on U.S. Expansion

## How do the sizes of the planets compare to the size of Earth?

**Project:** Make a Model of the Solar System

## How high is high?

**Project:** Compare Mountain Elevations

Name _____

☆ ☆
**Solve & Share**

Luke collected 1,034 baseball cards, 1,289 football cards, and 1,566 hockey cards. Use mental math to find the number of cards in Luke's collection. **Solve this problem any way you choose.**

**I can ...**
use properties and strategies to change a problem to add and subtract with mental math.

**I can also** make math arguments.

You can break apart the addends and use mental math to find the sum. *Show your work in the space below!*

**Look Back!** **Construct Arguments** How could you use mental math to solve 1,289 + 1,566? 1,034 + 1,566? How is the thinking different?

Essential Question

# How Can You Use Mental Math to Solve Problems?

**A**

Katy's dad washes windows at one of the tallest buildings in Miami, the Four Seasons Hotel. He worked Saturdays in October and earned more money than in September. How much did he earn in the two months combined?

You can use strategies based on properties to add numbers mentally.

Washing Windows
Earned $1,985 in Sept.
Earned $2,595 in Oct.

Find $1,985 + $2,595 with mental math.

---

**B Make Ten**

Break apart 1,985 to get a number that makes a ten, hundred, or thousand when added to 2,595. Then, use the **Associative Property of Addition** to change the grouping.

$1,985 + 2,595$
$= (1,580 + 405) + 2,595$
$= 1,580 + (405 + 2,595)$
$= 1,580 + 3,000$
$= 4,580$

Katy's dad earned $4,580.

---

**C Add On**

Break one addend apart and add on.

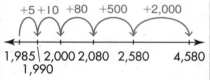

+5 +10  +80    +500      +2,000

1,985 | 2,000 2,080  2,580     4,580
1,990

You can start with either addend because of the **Commutative Property of Addition.**

+5 +80 +400   +500    +1,000

2,595 | 2,680 3,080  3,580    4,580
2,600

Katy's dad earned $4,580.

---

**D Use Compensation**

Add 15 to 1,985. Then subtract 15 from 2,595 to compensate. Adding 15 and subtracting 15 is the same as adding zero. Adding zero doesn't change the sum because of the **Identity Property of Addition.**

$1,985 + 2,595$
$= (1,985 + 15) + (2,595 - 15)$
$= 2,000 + 2,580$
$= 4,580$

Katy's dad earned $4,580.

---

**Convince Me!** **Use Structure** How could you make ten by breaking apart 2,595?

---

## Another Example!

Subtract 2,595 − 1,985 with mental math.

| Count Up | Count Down | Use Compensation |
|---|---|---|

### Count Up

Count from 1,985 up to 2,595.

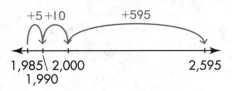

+5 +10      +595

1,985 2,000        2,595
1,990

Find how much you counted up.

5 + 10 + 595 = 610

### Count Down

Count down 1,985 from 2,595.

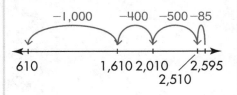

−1,000    −400  −500 −85

610        1,610 2,010  2,595
                2,510

### Use Compensation

Adding the same amount to both numbers in a subtraction problem doesn't change the difference.

(2,595 + 15) − (1,985 + 15)
= 2,610 − 2,000
= 610

## ☆ Guided Practice ☆

### Do You Understand?

1. Explain how to find 2,987 + 4,278 with mental math. What property does your strategy use?

### Do You Know How?

For **2-4**, use mental math strategies to solve.

2. 6,794 − 999

3. 4,505 + 3,515

4. 9,100 + 2,130 + 900

## Independent Practice ☆

For **5-10**, use mental math to solve.

5. 7,000 − 827

6. 1,225 + 975

7. 5,491 − 2,860

8. 6,686 − 1,443

9. 8,375 + 31,145

10. 23,100 + 74,900

# Problem Solving

For **11-12**, use the table at the right.

11. **Precision** How much greater is the area of California than Montana? Explain how to use mental math to solve.

12. Round the land area of the state with the least number of square miles to the nearest ten thousand.

| State | Square Miles of Land |
| --- | --- |
| Alaska | 570,641 |
| California | 155,779 |
| Montana | 145,546 |
| New Mexico | 121,298 |
| Texas | 261,232 |

13. The town of Worman Grove has collected 28,481 pens for a school supplies drive. Their goal is 30,000 pens. Show how to use counting on to find how many more pens they need to reach their goal.

14. Conservationists weigh two Northern elephant seals. An adult seal weighs 6,600 pounds, and its pup weighs 3,847 pounds. What is their combined weight? Explain how to use mental math to solve.

15. **Higher Order Thinking** Is Kelly's answer correct? What mistake did she make?

**Kelly's Work**

$5,356 + 2,398$

$= (5,356 + 2) + (2,398 + 2)$

$5,358 + 2,400 = 7,758$

## ✓ Assessment Practice

16. Use mental math to find $1,218 + 1,598$.

   Ⓐ  2,716

   Ⓑ  2,720

   Ⓒ  2,816

   Ⓓ  2,820

17. Use mental math to find $5,280 - 1,997$.

   Ⓐ  3,177

   Ⓑ  3,180

   Ⓒ  3,277

   Ⓓ  3,283

Name _____

☆ ☆
**Solve & Share**

A manufacturer in Detroit produces three new cars that weigh 6,127 pounds, 4,652 pounds, and 3,393 pounds. If these are are loaded on a truck, has the truck reached its 15,000-pound maximum? Use an estimate to decide. **Solve this problem any way you choose.**

## Lesson 2-2
### Estimate Sums and Differences

**I can ...**
use rounding and place value to estimate sums and differences.

**I can also** reason about math.

You can use reasoning and round each number to estimate the total weight.

**Look Back!** Why can you solve the problem using only an estimate rather than finding the exact weight of the three cars?

A

**Essential Question** **How Can You Estimate Sums and Differences of Whole Numbers?**

Books, magazines, and movies were checked out of the public library. About how many more books were checked out than magazines and movies combined?

Use reasoning. Use an estimate to solve. You can round to the nearest thousand or the nearest hundred to estimate.

12,642 books, 4,298 magazines, and 2,149 movies are checked out.

B
Estimate: Round to the nearest thousand.

Find the number of magazines and movies.

$$4{,}298 \longrightarrow 4{,}000$$
$$+\,2{,}149 \longrightarrow +\,2{,}000$$
$$\overline{\phantom{+\,2{,}149}\;6{,}000}$$

Subtract the number of magazines and movies from the rounded number of books.

$$13{,}000 - 6{,}000 = 7{,}000$$

About 7,000 more books were checked out.

C
Estimate: Round to the nearest hundred.

Find the number of magazines and movies.

$$4{,}298 \longrightarrow 4{,}300$$
$$+\,2{,}149 \longrightarrow +\,2{,}100$$
$$\overline{\phantom{+\,2{,}149}\;6{,}400}$$

Subtract the number of magazines and movies from the rounded number of books.

$$12{,}600 - 6{,}400 = 6{,}200$$

About 6,200 more books were checked out.

**Convince Me!** **Construct Arguments** The head librarian at the public library says she will establish a separate checkout desk for magazines and movies if the difference between the number of books and the number of these other materials is greater than 6,500. Which of the estimates above should you use to help her make her decision? Explain.

## Another Example!

Decide if each computation is reasonable.

You can use an estimate to decide whether or not an exact answer is reasonable.

$39,482 + 26,357 = 65,839$

39,482 + 26,357 is about 40,000 + 26,000 = 66,000

The sum, 65,839, is reasonable because it is close to the estimate of 66,000.

$8,215 - 5,852 = 3,643$

8,215 − 5,852 is about 8,000 − 6,000 = 2,000

The difference, 3,643, is not reasonable because it is not close to the estimate of 2,000.

## Guided Practice

### Do You Understand?

**1.** Is 2,793 a reasonable difference for 6,904 − 4,111? Explain.

### Do You Know How?

For **2–4**, estimate each sum or difference.

**2.**   5,638 ⟶ ☐,☐00
       + 3,753 ⟶ ☐,☐00

**3.**    63,526
        + 25,038

**4.**    262,262
        − 132,147

## Independent Practice

**Leveled Practice**  For **5–13**, estimate each sum or difference.

**5.**    5,323 ⟶  ☐,000
        + 2,611 ⟶ + ☐,000

**6.**    542,817 ⟶  ☐☐☐,☐00
        −  27,398 ⟶ −  ☐☐,☐00

**7.**    49,761 ⟶  ☐0,000
        + 59,499 ⟶ + ☐0,000

**8.**    4,225
        +    98

**9.**    738,775
        + 272,044

**10.**   24,300
        − 10,125

**11.** 485,635 − 231,957

**12.** 9,668 − 2,489

**13.** 368,545 + 114,254

# Problem Solving

14. The table shows the number of students at each school in the district. Is 2,981 reasonable for the total number of students at Wilson Elementary and Kwame Charter School? Explain.

| Numbers of Students in District 37 | |
|---|---|
| **School** | **Number of Students** |
| Wilson Elementary | 1,523 |
| Hearst Academy | 1,471 |
| Kwame Charter School | 1,458 |
| Evers Elementary | 1,697 |

DATA

15. **enVision® STEM** A satellite moves at a speed of 27,950 kilometers per hour. A satellite at a higher orbit travels at a speed of 11,190 kilometers per hour. About how much faster is one satellite than the other? Explain how to estimate.

16. **Critique Reasoning** Elle says, "When rounding to the nearest thousand, 928,674 rounds to 930,000." Do you agree? Explain.

17. **Higher Order Thinking** A football team needs to sell at least 20,000 tickets to two games to cover expenses. They sell 10,184 tickets to one game and 9,723 to the other. Estimate by rounding to the nearest thousand and by rounding to the nearest hundred. Did the team sell enough tickets? Explain your answer.

## ☑ Assessment Practice

18. Last week, Mallory flew two round trips. They were 3,720 miles and 5,985 miles. Which is the best estimate of the total distance Mallory flew?

    Ⓐ 11,000 miles

    Ⓑ 9,700 miles

    Ⓒ 8,700 miles

    Ⓓ 8,000 miles

19. Use estimation to decide which is a reasonable difference.

    38,041 − 19,558

    Ⓐ 21,374

    Ⓑ 20,973

    Ⓒ 18,473

    Ⓓ 16,483

Name_____

**Solve & Share**

Students collect empty plastic water bottles to recycle. How many bottles were collected in the first two months? How many bottles were collected in all three months? *Solve this problem using any strategy you choose.*

**I can ...**
connect place-value concepts to using addition algorithms.

**I can also** choose and use a math tool to help solve problems.

You can use appropriate tools, such as drawings or place-value blocks, to help you add.

| DATA | Month | Water Bottles |
|------|-----------|---------------|
| | September | 357 |
| | October | 243 |
| | November | 468 |

**Look Back!** When adding, how do you know when there are enough tens to make one hundred?

**Essential Question**

# How Do You Add Whole Numbers Efficiently?

**A**

*The Florida Legislature set a statewide recycling goal. To help meet this goal, Kennedy Elementary school students collected newspaper. How many pounds of newspaper did they collect in all?*

| DATA | Newspaper Collected | |
|---|---|---|
| | **Month** | **Pounds** |
| | March | 358 |
| | April | 277 |

Add 358 + 277.
Estimate.
350 + 250 = 600

*Connect adding partial sums to adding using the standard algorithm for addition.*

---

**B** **Add using partial sums.**

```
    358
  + 277
  ─────
     15    8 ones + 7 ones
    120    5 tens + 7 tens
  + 500    3 hundreds + 2 hundreds
  ─────
    635
```

**C** **Add using the standard algorithm.**

**Step 1**  Add ones.

```
     1
   358      8 ones + 7 ones = 15 ones
 + 277      Regroup. 15 ones = 1 ten + 5 ones
 ─────
       5
```

**Step 2**  Add tens.

```
   1 1
   358      5 tens + 7 tens + 1 ten = 13 tens
 + 277      Regroup: 13 tens =
 ─────
     35     1 hundred + 3 tens
```

**Step 3**  Add hundreds

```
   1 1
   358      3 hundreds +
 + 277      2 hundreds +
 ─────      1 hundred =
   635      6 hundreds
```

*The students collected 635 pounds of newspaper.*

---

**Convince Me!** **Use Structure** In the problem above, when you add partial sums you can add the ones first or the hundreds. Can you do the same when you add using the standard algorithm?

# ☆ Guided Practice

## Do You Understand?

**1.** When you place a 1 above the tens values, what does it mean?

**2.** When you place a 1 above the hundreds values, what does it mean?

## Do You Know How?

Find the sum by using partial sums and by using the standard algorithm.

**3.**   378
      + 557
     _____

Find each sum using the strategy you choose.

**4a.**   678        **b.**   325        **c.**   185
       + 253             + 256             + 253
      _____            _____            _____

# Independent Practice ☆

In **5–16**, find each sum.

**5.**    148
       + 157
      _____

**6.**    389
       + 461
      _____

**7.**    365
       + 458
      _____

**8.**    126
       + 138
      _____

**9.**    371
       + 454
      _____

**10.**    357
        + 498
       _____

**11.** 142 + 178

**12.** 565 + 694

**13.** 375 + 548

**14.** 718 + 865

**15.** 909 + 624

**16.** 129 + 587

**17. Construct Arguments** Harmony solved this problem using the standard algorithm, but she made an error. What was her error, and how can she fix it?

$$\begin{array}{r} \overset{1}{4}3\overset{}{7} \\ +\ 175 \\ \hline 5,112 \end{array}$$

**18. Higher Order Thinking** For which problems would you use a mental strategy or the standard algorithm to solve? Explain.

499 + 121

827 + 385

175 + 325

**19.** A Little League team played a doubleheader (two back-to-back baseball games). The first game lasted 155 minutes. The second game lasted 175 minutes. There was a 30-minute break between games. What was the total time of the doubleheader?

**Assessment Practice**

**20.** Select all the correct sums.

☐ 742 + 353 = 1,095
☐ 428 + 247 = 665
☐ 604 + 684 = 1,288
☐ 735 + 298 = 1,033
☐ 912 + 198 = 1,010

**21.** What is the missing digit in the addition problem?

$$\begin{array}{r} 3\ \square\ 5 \\ +\ 6\ 5\ 9 \\ \hline 1,0\ 0\ 4 \end{array}$$

Name _____

⭐ ⭐
**Solve & Share**

Erica's class collected 4,219 bottles for the recycling center. Ana's class collected 3,742 bottles. Leon's class collected 4,436 bottles. How many bottles did the three classes collect? *Solve this problem any way you choose.*

**I can ...**
use the standard algorithm and place value to add multi-digit numbers.

**I can also** generalize from examples.

Just like you did with smaller numbers, you can break up greater numbers by place value to help you add. *Show your work in the space below!*

**Look Back!** **Generalize** Which properties allow you to change the order and grouping of numbers to add? How did you use these properties?

**Essential Question** **How Do You Add Greater Numbers?**

**A**

*Plans for remodeling a sports stadium include adding an additional 19,255 seats. How many seats will be in the remodeled stadium?*

20,000 stadium seats
4,595 box seats

Seats in the original stadium:

$20,000 + 4,595 = 24,595$

You can use a variable to represent the unknown value. The variable, *s*, represents the total number of seats in the remodeled stadium.

You can use an algorithm which is a set of steps used to solve a math problem.

| *s* | |
|---|---|
| 24,595 | 19,255 |

**B** **Step 1**

Use the standard algorithm for addition.

To add $24,595 + 19,255$, add the ones, then the tens, and then the hundreds. Regroup if necessary.

$$\begin{array}{r} {}^{1\ 1}24,5\overset{}{9}5 \\ + 19,255 \\ \hline 850 \end{array}$$

**C** **Step 2**

Add the thousands and the ten thousands. Regroup if necessary.

$$\begin{array}{r} {}^{1}\ {}^{1\ 1}24,595 \\ + 19,255 \\ \hline 43,850 \end{array}$$

$s = 43,850$

The remodeled stadium will have 43,850 seats.

**D** **Step 3**

Use an estimate to check if your answer is reasonable.

$$\begin{array}{r} 24,595 \longrightarrow {}^{1}25,000 \\ + 19,255 \longrightarrow + 19,000 \\ \hline 44,000 \end{array}$$

43,850 is close to the estimate of 44,000, so the answer is reasonable.

You can add two or more numbers when you line up the numbers by place value. Add one place at a time.

**Convince Me!** **Construct Arguments** When using the standard algorithm to add $24,595 + 19,255$, how do you regroup 1 ten + 9 tens + 5 tens?

Name_____

☆ ★
Solve & Share

Carly's parents own a motel in Orlando with 224 rooms. Last night, 176 rooms were rented. How many rooms were not rented? **Solve this problem using any strategy you choose.**

I can ...
connect place-value concepts to using the standard algorithm for subtraction.

I can also look for patterns to solve problems.

You can use appropriate tools, such as place-value blocks, to help you subtract.

**Look Back!** How can you use properties to find the number of rooms not rented?

# How Can You Subtract Whole Numbers Efficiently?

**Visual Learning Bridge**

**A**

The movie theater already sold 172 seats. How many seats are still available?

Here's a way to record subtraction, called the *standard algorithm for subtraction.*

Seats 358 people

Subtract 358 − 172.

Estimate: 400 − 200 = 200

---

**B What You Show**

**Step 1** Subtract ones.

**Step 2** Subtract tens.

**Step 3** Subtract hundreds.

---

**C What You Write**

**Step 1** Subtract ones.

$$\begin{array}{r} 358 \\ -172 \\ \hline 6 \end{array}$$  8 ones − 2 ones = 6 ones

**Step 2** Subtract tens.

$$\begin{array}{r} {}^{2}\!3{}^{15}\!58 \\ -172 \\ \hline 86 \end{array}$$

Regroup: 3 hundreds + 5 tens
= 2 hundreds + 15 tens
15 tens − 7 tens = 8 tens

**Step 3** Subtract hundreds.

$$\begin{array}{r} {}^{2}\!3{}^{15}\!58 \\ -172 \\ \hline 186 \end{array}$$

2 hundreds − 1 hundred
= 1 hundred

The theater has 186 seats available.

The difference 186 is reasonable because it is close to the estimate of 200.

---

**Convince Me!** **Use Structure** How many times do you need to regroup to subtract 483 − 295? Explain.

# ☆ Guided Practice

## Do You Understand?

**1.** To subtract 859 − 583, how do you regroup 8 hundreds 5 tens?

**2.** What do you need to regroup to subtract 753 − 489 using the standard algorithm?

## Do You Know How?

In **3–6**, subtract. Use an estimate to check that your answer is reasonable.

**3.**   154
       −  89

**4.**   592
       − 357

**5.**   915
       − 288

**6.**   743
       − 694

# ☆ Independent Practice ☆

In **7–18**, subtract. Use an estimate to check that your answer is reasonable.

**7.**   289
       − 145

**8.**   326
       − 184

**9.**   736
       − 218

**10.**   525
        − 267

**11.**   683
        − 295

**12.**   847
        − 387

**13.**   475
        −  98

**14.**   826
        − 184

**15.**   936
        − 218

**16.** 167 − 79

**17.** 284 − 167

**18.** 817 − 548

## Problem Solving

**19.** How much greater is the area of Hernando County than Union County?

**20. Make Sense and Persevere** How much greater is the area of Monroe County than the area of Union County and Hernando County combined? Explain.

**Union County**
244 square miles

**Volusia County**
449 people per square mile

**Hernando County**
473 square miles

**Brevard County**
535 people per square mile

**Monroe County**
983 square miles

**21.** Population density is measured in people per square mile. It indicates how crowded an area is. How many more people per square mile does Brevard County have than neighboring Volusia County?

**22. Higher Order Thinking** What mistake did Leon make? What is the correct difference?

$$
\begin{array}{r}
\overset{6}{\cancel{7}}\overset{18}{\cancel{9}}\overset{13}{\cancel{3}} \\
-\ 5\ 7\ 6 \\
\hline
1\ 1\ 7
\end{array}
$$
Leon

---

### ✓ Assessment Practice

**23.** What is the difference?

$$
\begin{array}{r}
7\ 2\ 4 \\
-\ 4\ 5\ 9 \\
\hline
\end{array}
$$

Ⓐ 1,183

Ⓑ 335

Ⓒ 266

Ⓓ 265

**24.** What is the missing digit in the subtraction statement?

$$
\begin{array}{r}
6\ 3\ 4 \\
-\ 2\ \square\ 7 \\
\hline
3\ 3\ 7
\end{array}
$$

Name _____

## Solve & Share

Nevada has a land area of 109,781 square miles. Colorado has a land area of 103,642 square miles. How much larger is Nevada than Colorado? **Solve this problem any way you choose.**

**I can ...**
use the standard algorithm and place value to subtract whole numbers.

**I can also** look for patterns to solve problems.

You can use structure and break numbers apart by place value to subtract. *Show your work in the space below!*

**Look Back!** Estimate the difference in the areas of the two states. Is your answer close to this estimate?

**Essential Question** **How Do You Subtract Greater Numbers Efficiently?**

**A**

*Three of the country's most scenic national parks are in Alaska. How much larger is the area of Gates of the Arctic than the combined area of Denali and Kenai Fjords?*

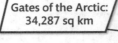 Gates of the Arctic: 34,287 sq km

 Denali: 19,182 sq km

Kenai Fjord: 2,711 sq km

Find the total area of Denali and Kenai Fjords.

$$\begin{array}{r} 19{,}182 \\ +\ \ 2{,}711 \\ \hline 21{,}893 \end{array} \text{ square kilometers}$$

Then find the difference of the areas.

| 34,287 | |
|--------|-------|
| 21,893 | *a* |

Let *a* equal the difference in the areas.

**B Step 1**

Find 34,287 − 21,893.

Subtract the ones. Regroup if necessary.

$$\begin{array}{r} 34{,}287 \\ -\ 21{,}893 \\ \hline 4 \end{array}$$

**C Step 2**

Subtract the tens, hundreds, thousands, and ten thousands.

Regroup if necessary.

$$\begin{array}{r} \overset{3\ \ 1118}{3\cancel{4}{,}2\cancel{8}7} \\ -\ 21{,}893 \\ \hline 12{,}394 \end{array}$$

Gates of the Arctic is 12,394 square kilometers larger.

**D Step 3**

Operations that undo each other are inverse operations. Addition and subtraction have an inverse relationship. Add to check your answer.

$$\begin{array}{r} \overset{1\ \ 1}{12{,}394} \\ +\ 21{,}893 \\ \hline 34{,}287 \end{array}$$

**Convince Me!** **Critique Reasoning** The work shown is **NOT** correct. What errors were made? Show how to find the correct answer.

$$\begin{array}{r} \overset{14}{4{,}2\cancel{4}8} \\ -\ 2{,}764 \\ \hline 2{,}584 \end{array}$$

Name_____

**Solve & Share**

London, England, is 15,710 kilometers from the South Pole. Tokyo, Japan, is 13,953 kilometers from the South Pole. How much farther is London than Tokyo from the South Pole? **Solve this problem any way you choose.**

**I can ...**
use the standard algorithm to subtract from numbers with zeros.

**I can also** reason about math.

You can use reasoning to identify the operation you use to compare two distances. *Show your work in the space below!*

**Look Back!** Explain how you decided what operation to use to find how much farther London is than Tokyo from the South Pole.

**Essential Question: How Do You Subtract Across Zeros?**

**A**

A music hall is hosting a concert. The hall sells 4,678 tickets to the show. How many tickets are still available?

When subtracting from a number with zeros, you may need to regroup several places before subtracting.

Let *t* equal the number of available tickets.

6,000 seats

| 6,000 | |
|---|---|
| 4,678 | *t* |

$t = 6,000 - 4,678$

Estimate: $6,000 - 4,700 = 1,300$

**B** **Regroup.**

6,000
− 4,678

Because of the zeros, you need to start regrouping from the thousands.

5 10
6,000
− 4,678

6 thousands = 5 thousands + 10 hundreds

5 9 10 10
6,000
− 4,678

10 hundreds = 9 hundreds + 10 tens

5 9 9 10 10 10
6,000
− 4,678

10 tens = 9 tens + 10 ones

**C** **Subtract.**

5 9 9 10 10 10
6,000
− 4,678
1,3 2 2

10 − 8 = 2 ones
90 − 70 = 20 = 2 tens
900 − 600 = 300 = 3 hundreds
5,000 − 4,000 = 1,000 = 1 thousand

Since the difference 1,322 is close to the estimate 1,300, the difference is reasonable.

There are still 1,322 tickets available for the concert.

**Convince Me! Use Structure** How would you regroup if the hall had 5,900 seats?

Name _____

# ☆Guided Practice

## Do You Understand?

**1.** Leesa used compensation to solve the problem on the previous page. She subtracted (6,000 − 1) − (4,678 − 1) = 5,999 − 4,677 = 1,322. How could you use Leesa's approach to subtract 5,000 − 1,476?

**2.** One passenger flew 11,033 kilometers from Oslo to Lima. Another passenger flew 8,593 kilometers from Oslo to Los Angeles. How many more kilometers was the flight to Lima?

## Do You Know How?

For **3–8**, subtract.

| | | | |
|---|---|---|---|
| **3.** | 6,000<br>− 1,773 | **4.** | 231,086<br>− 172,863 |
| **5.** | 76,810<br>− 22,645 | **6.** | 90,304<br>− 51,137 |

**7.** 101,001 − 8,915   **8.** 9,050 − 3,461

# Independent Practice ☆

For **9–23**, subtract.

Estimate to check if your answer is reasonable.

| | | | |
|---|---|---|---|
| **9.** 1,902<br>− 1,374 | **10.** 6,502<br>− 5,380 | **11.** 63,000<br>− 48,673 | **12.** 84,010<br>− 3,992 |
| **13.** 2,025<br>− 1,540 | **14.** 31,030<br>− 27,426 | **15.** 50,469<br>− 22,917 | **16.** 1,830<br>− 644 |
| **17.** 7,203<br>− 847 | **18.** 726,003<br>− 282,942 | **19.** 4,707<br>− 2,016 | **20.** 30,900<br>− 22,855 |

**21.** 6,090 − 5,130     **22.** 11,246 − 9,489     **23.** 790,008 − 643,829

# Problem Solving

**24. Construct Arguments** Will the difference between 44,041 and 43,876 be greater or less than 1,000? Explain.

**25.**  **Vocabulary** Define *variable* and give an example of how a variable is used in an equation.

For **26–27**, use the table at the right.

**26.** How many more hip-hop than country downloads were sold?

**27. Higher Order Thinking** How many more hip-hop and Latin downloads were sold than rock and country downloads? Explain.

DATA

**Music City Sales**

| Music style | Downloads sold |
| --- | --- |
| Rock | 4,007 |
| Hip-hop | 7,097 |
| Country | 5,063 |
| Latin | 6,203 |

## Assessment Practice

**28.** Select all the correct differences.

- ☐ 5,000 − 1,856 = 3,244
- ☐ 10,700 − 8,243 = 2,457
- ☐ 64,002 − 43,178 = 20,934
- ☐ 98,000 − 59,214 = 38,786
- ☐ 600,482 − 428,531 = 171,951

**29.** Find the difference.

$$60,000$$
$$- 38,243$$

- Ⓐ 17,355
- Ⓑ 20,757
- Ⓒ 21,757
- Ⓓ 98,243

Name _____

**Solve & Share**

A group of students collected donations for a toy drive. They collected a total of 3,288 toys one week and 1,022 toys the next week. They donated 1,560 toys to the Coal City Charity and the rest were donated to Hartville Charity. How many toys were donated to Hartville Charity? Use reasoning about numbers to show and explain how the two quantities of toys given to charity are related.

**I can ...**
make sense of quantities and relationships in problem situations.

**I can also** solve multi-step problems.

### Thinking Habits

*Be a good thinker!*
*These questions can help you.*

- What do the numbers and symbols in the problem mean?

- How are the numbers or quantities related?

- How can I represent a word problem using pictures, numbers, or equations?

**Look Back!** **Reasoning** Over three weeks, the students collected a total of 8,169 toys. How many toys did they collect in the third week? Complete the bar diagram to show your reasoning. Did the students collect more toys in the third week than in weeks 1 and 2 combined? Explain.

| | |
|---|---|
| | |

**Essential Question**

## How Can You Use Quantitative Reasoning to Solve Problems?

**Visual Learning Bridge**

**A**

*Kara and Carl join their mother on a boat off the coast of the Florida Keys. Their mother is a scientist studying blue marlins. Each child gets to help weigh two marlins. How much more did Kara's marlins weigh than Carl's?*

**How can you draw a diagram to help reason how the numbers in the problem are related?**

I can represent the relationship between the numbers with a bar diagram.

*Here's my thinking.*

| DATA | Kara's Marlins | Carl's Marlins |
| --- | --- | --- |
| | 948 pounds | 895 pounds |
| | 1,219 pounds | 973 pounds |

**B**

**How can I use reasoning to solve this problem?**

**I can**

- identify the quantities I know.

- draw diagrams and write equations to show relationships.

- connect the solution back to the real world problem.

**C**

$K$ = the total weight of Kara's marlins, and $C$ = the total weight of Carl's marlins.

$K$

| 948 lb | 1,219 lb |
| --- | --- |

$K = 948 + 1,219$
$K = 2,167$

$C$

| 895 lb | 973 lb |
| --- | --- |

$C = 895 + 973$
$C = 1,868$

$d$ = the difference
$d = 2,167 - 1,868$
$d = 299$

| $K = 2,167$ | |
| --- | --- |
| $C = 1,868$ | $d$ |

Kara's marlins weighed 299 pounds more than Carl's.

---

**Convince Me!** **Reasoning** Write a problem that can be solved using the bar diagram below. Write an equation to solve. Use reasoning to think about the meaning of each number before starting.

16,792

| 2,550 | $c$ |
| --- | --- |

# Guided Practice

### Reasoning

A manufacturer shipped 12,875 fidget spinners one week and 9,843 of them were sold. The next week, they shipped 19,175 and 12,752 of them were sold. How many fidget spinners had not sold yet?

When you use reasoning, you use diagrams, numbers, or equations to show relationships.

1. What quantities are given in the problem, and what do the numbers mean?

2. Use the bar diagrams that show the relationships of the numbers in the problem. Write and solve equations which could be used to find $f$, the spinners not sold the first week; $s$, the spinners not sold the second week; and $t$, the total spinners not sold.

# Independent Practice

### Reasoning

A wall is being built with 16,351 stones. The builders have placed 8,361 stones, and they have 7,944 stones left. Do they have enough stones? How many more stones do they need? Use Exercises 3–5 to answer the question.

3. What quantities are given in the problem, and what do the numbers mean?

4. Complete the bar diagram to show how to find $s$, the number of stones the builders have in all. Then, write and solve an equation. Do they have enough? Explain.

5. Complete the bar diagram to show how to find the difference, $d$, of how many more stones the builders need. Then, write and solve an equation.

## Problem Solving

✅ **Performance Task**

**Bird Migration**
Ornithology is the scientific study of birds. Every year, some birds travel great distances, or migrate, to find food and start families. The table shows the distances five species of birds flew over one year, as observed by an ornithologist. How much farther did the Arctic Tern fly than the Pectoral Sandpiper and the Pied Wheatear combined?

**Distances Traveled by Birds**

| Species | Distance in Miles |
| --- | --- |
| Sooty Shearwater | 39,481 |
| Pied Wheatear | 11,184 |
| Arctic Tern | 44,819 |
| Short-Tailed Shearwater | 26,636 |
| Pectoral Sandpiper | 18,247 |

6. **Reasoning** What quantities are given in the problem and what do the numbers mean?

7. **Make Sense and Persevere** What strategy can you use to solve the problem?

The hidden questions are the questions which must be answered before answering the main question asked in the problem.

8. **Make Sense and Persevere** What is the hidden question?

9. **Model with Math** Complete the bar diagrams to show how to find the answer to the hidden question and the main question. Write and solve equations.

Name _____

Shade a path from **START** to **FINISH**. Follow the sums that are correct. You can only move up, down, right, or left.

**Fluency Practice Activity**

**I can ...**
add multi-digit whole numbers.

**I can also** be precise in my work.

| Start | | | | |
|---|---|---|---|---|
| 213<br>+ 675<br>**888** | 264<br>+ 632<br>**896** | 887<br>+ 112<br>**999** | 124<br>+ 345<br>**461** | 414<br>+ 111<br>**515** |
| 810<br>+ 172<br>**762** | 212<br>+ 486<br>**678** | 511<br>+ 228<br>**739** | 245<br>+ 322<br>**667** | 613<br>+ 282<br>**891** |
| 454<br>+ 545<br>**919** | 187<br>+ 412<br>**499** | 676<br>+ 322<br>**998** | 101<br>+ 116<br>**218** | 454<br>+ 432<br>**876** |
| 409<br>+ 390<br>**697** | 340<br>+ 340<br>**620** | 124<br>+ 65<br>**189** | 911<br>+ 64<br>**975** | 674<br>+ 115<br>**789** |
| 374<br>+ 613<br>**978** | 318<br>+ 121<br>**429** | 177<br>+ 311<br>**478** | 612<br>+ 317<br>**939** | 678<br>+ 321<br>**999** |

Finish

## TOPIC 2 — Vocabulary Review

Glossary

**Word List**

- add on
- algorithm
- Associative Property of Addition
- Commutative Property of Addition
- compensation
- Identity Property of Addition
- inverse operations
- variable

### Understand Vocabulary

**1.** Circle the property of addition shown by $126 + 0 = 126$.

    Associative         Commutative         Identity

**2.** Circle the property of addition shown by $21 + 34 = 34 + 21$.

    Associative         Commutative         Identity

**3.** Circle the property of addition shown by $(1 + 3) + 7 = 1 + (3 + 7)$.

    Associative         Commutative         Identity

**4.** Draw a line from each term to its example.

| Term | Example |
|------|---------|
| algorithm | $4 + 2 = 6 \longrightarrow 6 - 2 = 4$ |
| compensation | $435 - 199 = (435 + 1) - (199 + 1)$ |
| add on | Step 1: Add the ones.<br>Step 2: Add the tens. |
| inverse operations | $x = 7$ |
| variable | $326 + 103$: $326 + 3 = 329$,<br>$329 + 100 = 429$ |

### Use Vocabulary in Writing

**5.** Rob found $103 + 1,875 = x$ using mental math. Use at least 3 terms from the Word List to describe how Rob could find the sum.

**Set A** pages 37–40

Find 3,371 + 2,429. Use mental math.

Make Ten

$$3{,}371 + 2{,}429 = 3{,}371 + (29 + 2{,}400)$$
$$= (3{,}371 + 29) + 2{,}400$$
$$= 3{,}400 + 2{,}400 = 5{,}800$$

So, 3,371 + 2,429 = 5,800.

**Reteaching**

**Remember** to adjust the sum or difference when you use the compensation strategy.

**1.** 4,153 + 2,988    **2.** 92,425 + 31,675

**3.** 5,342 + 1,999    **4.** 22,283 − 14,169

**5.** 47,676 − 16,521    **6.** 1,089 − 961

**Set B** pages 41–44

Estimate the sum by rounding each number to the nearest ten thousand.

$$\begin{array}{r} 241{,}485 \\ +\,429{,}693 \\ \hline \end{array}$$

241,485 rounds to 240,000.

429,693 rounds to 430,000.

Add.
$$\begin{array}{r} 240{,}000 \\ +\,430{,}000 \\ \hline 670{,}000 \end{array}$$

**Remember** that you can round numbers to any place when estimating sums and differences.

Estimate each sum or difference.

**1.** 652,198 + 49,753    **2.** 8,352 − 3,421

**3.** 17,586 − 9,483    **4.** 823,725 + 44,851

**5.** 1,440 − 933    **6.** 55,748 − 28,392

**7.** 4,981 + 6,193    **8.** 995,275 + 4,921

**Set C** pages 45–52

Find 72,438 + 6,854.

Estimate: 72,000 + 7,000 = 79,000

Add the ones. Regroup if necessary.

$$\begin{array}{r} \overset{1}{7}2{,}43\overset{}{8} \\ +\ \ 6{,}854 \\ \hline 2 \end{array}$$

Add the other places, regrouping if necessary.

$$\begin{array}{r} 7\overset{1}{2}{,}4\overset{1}{3}8 \\ +\ \ 6{,}854 \\ \hline 79{,}292 \end{array}$$

The answer 79,292 is close to the estimate of 79,000, so the answer is reasonable.

**Remember** to regroup if necessary when adding whole numbers.

**1.**  $\begin{array}{r} 32{,}834 \\ +\,17{,}384 \\ \hline \end{array}$    **2.**  $\begin{array}{r} 148{,}382 \\ +\ \ \ 9{,}243 \\ \hline \end{array}$

**3.** 215 + 8,823    **4.** 142,968 + 44,456

**5.** 2,417 + 3,573    **6.** 572,941 + 181,662

## Set D | pages 53–60

Find 52,839 − 38,796.

Estimate: 53,000 − 39,000 = 14,000

Subtract the ones. Regroup if necessary.

$$\begin{array}{r} 52,83\overset{}{9} \\ -\ 38,796 \\ \hline 3 \end{array}$$

Subtract the other places, regrouping as necessary.

$$\begin{array}{r} \overset{4\ 12\ \ 7\ 13}{\cancel{5}2,\cancel{8}\cancel{3}9} \\ -\ 38,796 \\ \hline 14,043 \end{array}$$

The answer is reasonable.

**Remember** that you may need to regroup to subtract.

1. $\begin{array}{r} 651,784 \\ -\ 482,638 \\ \hline \end{array}$    2. $\begin{array}{r} 18,465 \\ -\ 6,291 \\ \hline \end{array}$

3. 41,542 − 32,411    4. 4,978 − 2,766

5. 735,184 − 255,863    6. 44,558 − 22,613

## Set E | pages 61–64

Find 60,904 − 54,832.

Estimate: 61,000 − 55,000 = 6,000

Subtract the ones. Regroup if necessary.

$$\begin{array}{r} 60,904 \\ -\ 54,832 \\ \hline 2 \end{array}$$

Subtract the other places, regrouping as necessary.

$$\begin{array}{r} \overset{5\ 10\ \ 8\ 10}{\cancel{6}\cancel{0},\cancel{9}\cancel{0}4} \\ -\ 54,832 \\ \hline 6,072 \end{array}$$

The answer is reasonable.

**Remember** you may need to regroup more than one place at a time to subtract across zeros.

1. $\begin{array}{r} 40,700 \\ -\ 23,984 \\ \hline \end{array}$    2. $\begin{array}{r} 203,056 \\ -\ 5,213 \\ \hline \end{array}$

3. 70,000 − 25,228    4. 560,043 − 312,562

5. 8,052 − 1,205    6. 20,008 − 16,074

## Set F | pages 65–68

Think about these questions to help you **reason abstractly and quantitatively.**

### Thinking Habits

- What do the numbers and symbols in the problem mean?

- How are the numbers or quantities related?

- How can I represent a word problem using pictures, numbers, or equations?

**Remember** that you can draw a bar diagram and use it to reason about a problem.

Raahil traveled 11,469 kilometers from home to visit his mother's family in Qatar. He then traveled 12,332 kilometers from Qatar to visit his father's family in Brisbane, Australia.

1. Draw a bar diagram that shows the distance Raahil traveled to Brisbane.

2. Write and solve an equation for your bar diagram.

Name_____

**Taking Inventory**

Jiao runs a wholesale art supply website. She fills bulk orders for craft and hobby stores.

1. Use the **Wooden Beads** table to answer the questions.

**Part A**

Crafts and Stuff ordered oak and ebony beads. Explain how to use mental math and properties of addition to find how many beads Jiao sent.

| Wooden Beads | |
| --- | --- |
| Oak | 4,525 |
| Maple | 6,950 |
| Ash | 3,720 |
| Ebony | 2,475 |
| Bayong | 1,250 |

**Part B**

Jiao sends an order of oak and bayong beads to Jill's Crafts and an order of ash and ebony beads to Create. How much larger is the order for Create? Write and solve equations to find $j$, the number of beads in the order to Jill's Crafts; $c$, the number of beads in the order to Create; and $d$, the difference.

**2.** Use the **Glass Beads** table to answer the questions.

**Part A**

Write and solve an equation to show how many glass beads, *b*, Create will have if they order the bubble and smoky beads.

| Glass Beads | |
| --- | --- |
| Smoky | 25,236 |
| Bubble | 41,828 |
| Stained | 32,991 |
| Molded | 47,312 |

**Part B**

Jiao sends the molded and stained beads to Hometown Craft Supply. Explain how to use compensation to find how many more molded beads than stained beads were sent.

**3.** Use the **Metal Beads** table to answer the questions.

**Part A**

Write and solve an equation to show how many more beads, *b*, are in an order of gold beads than in an order of platinum beads.

| Metal Beads | |
| --- | --- |
| Gold | 14,960 |
| Silver | 8,147 |
| Platinum | 6,488 |
| Brass | 30,019 |
| Copper | 20,605 |

**Part B**

Craftology orders the brass and copper beads. After they arrive, the store sells 29,735 of them. How many beads does Craftology have left from their order? Show your computations.

# Use Strategies and Properties to Multiply by 1-Digit Numbers

**Essential Questions:** How can you multiply by multiples of 10, 100, and 1,000? How can you multiply whole numbers?

**Digital Resources**

Interactive Student Edition    Activity    Visual Learning    Video    Practice

Assessment    Games    Tools    Glossary

Maps that show the natural features of Earth's landscape are called topographic maps. Mountains, plains, and oceans are some of the features the maps show.

Did you know that Pikes Peak is the most visited mountain in North America?

We should visit! In the meantime, here is a project on maps and multiplication.

## enVision STEM Project: Maps and Math

**Do Research** Use the Internet or other sources to find information about three of Earth's features on a topographic map, such as mountains or oceans. Write two facts about each of the features you researched.

**Journal: Write a Report** Include what you found. Also in your report:

- Write the height or depth of each feature you researched.

- Estimate to find 10 times the heights or depths of the features you researched.

Name_____

# Review What You Know

**A-Z Vocabulary**

Choose the best term from the box. Write it on the blank.

| |
|---|
| • breaking apart • inverse operations |
| • compensation • partial products |

1. Multiplication and division are

   _____.

2. A mental math method used to rewrite a number as the sum of numbers to form an easier problem is called _____.

3. Choosing numbers close to the numbers in a problem to make the computation easier, and then adjusting the answer is called _____.

## Multiplication

Find each product.

**4.** $6 \times 2$  **5.** $8 \times 9$  **6.** $6 \times 5$

**7.** $7 \times 8$  **8.** $4 \times 8$  **9.** $3 \times 7$

## Rounding

Round each number to the nearest ten.

**10.** 16  **11.** 82  **12.** 35

**13.** 53  **14.** 24  **15.** 49

Round each number to the nearest hundred.

**16.** 868  **17.** 499  **18.** 625

**19.** 167  **20.** 341  **21.** 772

**22.** 919  **23.** 552  **24.** 321

## Problem Solving

**25. Critique Reasoning** Tyler says, "$9 \times 7$ is greater than $7 \times 9$ because the greater number is first." Explain Tyler's error.

Name

## PROJECT 3A

**How zesty is Key lime pie?**

**Project:** Create Data for Key Lime Pie Ingredients

## PROJECT 3B

**What do a dozen Florida panthers weigh?**

**Project:** Draw a Captioned Picture

## PROJECT 3C

**What's the mass of a giraffe?**

**Project:** Create a Song

Before watching the video, think:

Every box has three dimensions: length, width, and height. How much paper you need to wrap the box depends on all three of the dimensions. There are also other shapes you can wrap. I just wish someone had told me this wasn't a birthday party!

## I can ...
model with math to solve a problem that involves estimating and computing with area models.

Name_____

 Activity

Solve & Share

Find the products for 3 × 4, 3 × 40, 3 × 400, and 3 × 4,000. **Solve these problems using any strategy you choose.**

**I can ...**
find the products of multiples of 10, 100, and 1,000 using mental math and place-value strategies.

**I can also** look for patterns to solve problems.

You can look for relationships in the products. How can finding the first product help you find the remaining products?

**Look Back!** What pattern do you notice in the products?

**Essential Question** **How Can You Multiply by Multiples of 10, 100, and 1,000?**

**A**

*Calculate 3 × 50, 3 × 500, and 3 × 5,000 using basic multiplication facts and properties of operations.*

The Associative Property of Multiplication states that you can change the grouping of the factors and the product stays the same.

$n$

---

**B** **One Way**

Find 3 × 50, 3 × 500, and 3 × 5,000.

Use basic facts and place value.

$3 \times 50 = 3 \times 5$ tens
$\qquad = 15$ tens
$\qquad = 150$

$3 \times 500 = 3 \times 5$ hundreds
$\qquad = 15$ hundreds
$\qquad = 1,500$

$3 \times 5,000 = 3 \times 5$ thousands
$\qquad = 15$ thousands
$\qquad = 15,000$

**C** **Another Way**

Find 3 × 50, 3 × 500, and 3 × 5,000.

Break apart numbers. Use the Associative Property of Multiplication.

$3 \times 50 = 3 \times (5 \times 10)$
$\qquad = (3 \times 5) \times 10$
$\qquad = 15 \times 10$
$\qquad = 150$

$3 \times 500 = 3 \times (5 \times 100)$
$\qquad = (3 \times 5) \times 100$
$\qquad = 15 \times 100$
$\qquad = 1,500$

$3 \times 5,000 = 3 \times (5 \times 1,000)$
$\qquad = (3 \times 5) \times 1,000$
$\qquad = 15 \times 1,000$
$\qquad = 15,000$

---

**Convince Me!** **Reasoning** What patterns do you see in the number of zeros in the products above?

Name _____

Practice  Tools  Assessment

## Another Example!

Use place value to calculate 5 × 400 and 6 × 5,000.

5 × 400 = 5 × 4 hundreds          6 × 5,000 = 6 × 5 thousands
        = 20 hundreds                        = 30 thousands
        = 2,000                              = 30,000

If the product of the basic fact ends in zero, the product has one more zero than you see in the factors.

## ☆ Guided Practice

### Do You Understand?

1. Show how you can use the basic fact 5 × 8 = 40 to determine the product of 5 × 800.

2. Bob said 4 × 500 = 200. Explain his error using place value.

### Do You Know How?

For **3–5**, use strategies you learned to help multiply.

3. 8 × 7 = _____

   8 × 70 = _____

   8 × 700 = _____

   8 × 7,000 = _____

4. 7 × 70

5. 2 × 700

## ☆ Independent Practice ☆

You can use place-value strategies to calculate each product.

**Leveled Practice** For **6–11**, use basic facts, place value, and properties to help multiply.

6. 3 × 70 = _____          7. _____ = 6 × 40          8. 8 × 50 = _____

   3 × 700 = _____            _____ = 6 × 400            8 × 500 = _____

   3 × 7,000 = _____          _____ = 6 × 4,000          8 × 5,000 = _____

9. 4 × 2,000          10. 700 × 4          11. 6 × 60

# Problem Solving

12. **enVision® STEM** The Mississippi River is about 8 times the length of the Hudson River. If the Hudson River is about 300 miles long, about how many miles long is the Mississippi River? Write and solve an equation.

13. Ted, Jason, and Angelina are trying to raise $200 for a local shelter. Ted raised $30. Jason raised $90. How much money, *m*, does Angelina need to raise to reach their goal?

| $200 | | |
|------|------|------|
| $30 | $90 | *m* |

For **14–15**, use the table at the right.

14. **Make Sense and Persevere** There are 9 girls and 4 adults in Aimee's scout troup. How much did the troop pay for tickets to the amusement park?

15. **Higher Order Thinking** Tina visited Funland with her mom and a friend. They bought tickets for Plan C. How much money did they save on the two children's tickets for Plan C instead of buying separate tickets for Plan A and Plan B?

**Funland Ticket Prices**

| Plans | Adult | Child |
|-------|-------|-------|
| Plan A Waterpark | $30 | $20 |
| Plan B Amusement Park | $40 | $30 |
| Plan C Combined A + B | $60 | $40 |

## Assessment Practice

16. Brandon says 4 × 800 is greater than 8 × 4,000. Renee says 4 × 800 is less than 8 × 4,000.

**A.**

Without calculating the answer, explain how to use place-value strategies or the Associative Property to find which is greater.

**B.**

Without calculating the answer, explain how to use relationships or basic facts to find which is less.

Name_____

Activity

## Solve & Share

Sarah earns $48 a week babysitting. She saves all of her earnings for 6 weeks. Estimate to determine about how much money Sarah saves. **Solve this problem using any strategy you choose.**

**I can ...** use rounding to estimate products and check if my answer is reasonable.

**I can also** reason about math.

How can reasoning about place value make it easier to estimate products? *Show your work in the space above!*

**Look Back!** Is your estimate more or less than the amount Sarah actually earned? Explain.

**Essential Question** **How Can You Estimate When You Multiply?**

**A**

*Mr. Hector's class sold calendars and note pads for 3 weeks as a class fundraiser. About how much did Mr. Hector's class make selling calendars? selling note pads?*

Note Pads $3

Calendars $4

**DATA**

| Item | Number Sold Week 1 | Number Sold Week 2 | Number Sold Week 3 |
|---|---|---|---|
| Calendar | 28 | 73 | 63 |
| Note Pads | 272 | 475 | 232 |

**B** Use compatible numbers to estimate how many calendars $c$, were sold.

$28 + 73 + 63 = c$
$\qquad 164 = c$

Estimate $\$4 \times 164$.

```
          164
◄──┼────────┼────────┼──►
  100      150      200
```

Estimate by using compatible numbers. 164 is close to 150.

$4 \times 150 = 600$

Mr. Hector's class made about $600 selling calendars.

**C** Use rounding to estimate how many note pads $n$, were sold.

$272 + 475 + 232 = n$
$\qquad 979 = n$

Estimate $\$3 \times 979$.

```
                       979
◄──┼────────┼────────┼┼─►
   0       500     1,000
```

To the nearest thousand, 979 rounds to 1,000.

$3 \times 1,000 = 3,000$

Mr. Hector's class made about $3,000 selling note pads.

**Convince Me!** **Construct Arguments** Could you solve the problem above by rounding to estimate the total number of calendars and the total number of note pads? Explain.

## Another Example!

Mrs. Li's class made $2,089 selling neon pencil packs. A student calculated that Mr. Hector's class and Mrs. Li's class together made $8,865 selling the school supplies. Is the student's calculation reasonable?

You can estimate to check if an answer is reasonable.

Round Mrs. Li's total to the nearest thousand: $2,000. Then, add the rounded amounts. $2,000 + $600 + $3,000 = $5,600

The student's calculation is not reasonable because $8,865 is not close to $5,600.

## ☆ Guided Practice

### Do You Understand?

1. Mr. Harm's class sold 1,275 items at $5 per item. One of his students calculates the class raised $2,375. Is the student's calculation reasonable? Explain.

### Do You Know How?

For **2–5**, estimate the product.

**2.** $6 \times 125$        **3.** $4 \times 2,610$

**4.** $538 \times 3$        **5.** $314 \times 7$

## Independent Practice ☆

**Leveled Practice** For **6–8**, estimate the product.

**6.** $3 \times 287$
↓ Round 287 to _____.
$3 \times$ _____ = _____

**7.** $6 \times 1,310$
↓ Round 1,310 to _____.
$6 \times$ _____ = _____

**8.** $9 \times 62$
↓ Round 62 to _____.
$9 \times$ _____ = _____

For **9–11**, estimate to check if the answer is reasonable.

**9.** $7 \times 486 = 3,402$
↓ Round 486 to _____.
$7 \times$ _____ = _____

Reasonable   Not Reasonable

**10.** $5 \times 1,240 = 9,200$
↓ Round 1,240 to _____.
$5 \times$ _____ = _____

Reasonable   Not Reasonable

**11.** $9 \times 287 = 2,583$
↓ Round 287 to _____.
$9 \times$ _____ = _____

Reasonable   Not Reasonable

# Problem Solving

For **12–13**, use the graph at the right.

12. The students voted on a school mascot. Which mascot had 4 times as many of votes as the flamingo?

13. **Construct Arguments** Explain how you could estimate the number of students who voted on a school mascot. Then give your estimate.

**School Mascot Votes**

14. **Number Sense** Ellie says the product of 211 and 6 is 1,866. Is this calculation reasonable? Explain.

15. **Higher Order Thinking** An adult sleeps about 480 minutes per day. An infant sleeps about 820 minutes per day. About how many more minutes does an infant sleep than an adult in one week? Solve the problem two different ways.

## Assessment Practice

16. Gul can run 800 meters in 139 seconds. About how long would it take her to run 6 times as far if she runs at the same speed? Choose the best estimate.

    Ⓐ  About 140 seconds

    Ⓑ  About 600 seconds

    Ⓒ  About 1,200 seconds

    Ⓓ  About 6,000 seconds

17. A new two-seater car weighs 1,785 pounds. About how much would 8 of the two-seater cars weigh? Choose the best estimate.

    Ⓐ  About 160 pounds

    Ⓑ  About 1,600 pounds

    Ⓒ  About 16,000 pounds

    Ⓓ  About 60,000 pounds

Name_____

## Solve & Share

A music room has chairs arranged in rows. There are 6 rows. Each row has 18 chairs. How many chairs are in the music room? **Solve this problem any way you choose.** Explain your answer.

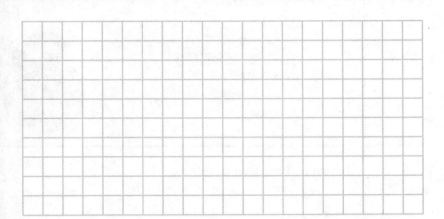

**I can ...**
use arrays and partial products to multiply.

**I can also** model with math to solve problems.

You can model with math. You can represent how the chairs are arranged to help solve the problem. *Show your work in the space above!*

**Look Back!** Would the answer be different if there were 18 rows with 6 chairs in each row? Explain.

Visual Learning  A-Z Glossary

## How Can You Use an Array and Partial Products to Multiply?

**Essential Question**

Visual Learning Bridge

**A** The windows of a building on International Drive are in an array. There are 5 rows with 13 windows in each row. How many windows are in this array?

**B What You Show**

13 windows per row

5 rows

An array is an arrangement of objects in equal rows.

**C What You Think**

Find $5 \times 13$.

Estimate: $5 \times 13$ is about $5 \times 10 = 50$.

5 rows, 1 ten in each
$5 \times 10 = 50$

5 rows, 3 ones in each
$5 \times 3 = 15$

$50 + 15 = 65$

The numbers 15 and 50 are called **partial products**. 65 is the product.

**D What You Record**

$$
\begin{array}{r}
13 \\
\times\ 5 \\
\hline
15 \\
+\ 50 \\
\hline
65
\end{array}
$$

$5 \times 3$ ones
$5 \times 1$ ten

There are 65 windows in the array.

The product, 65, is close to the estimate of 50. The answer is reasonable.

You can use place value to break factors apart and the Distributive Property to find partial products.

**Convince Me! Use Structure** How are the partial products represented with the place-value blocks?

**90 Topic 3** | Lesson 3-3

## Another Example!

Find $2 \times 126$.

Estimate:
$2 \times 126$ is about $2 \times 100 = 200$.

You can find partial products for hundreds, tens, and ones.

$$
\begin{array}{r}
126 \\
\times\ \ 2 \\
\hline
\end{array}
$$

partial products

200   $2 \times 1$ hundred
40   $2 \times 2$ tens
+ 12   $2 \times 6$ ones
____
252

2 rows, 1 hundred in each      2 rows, 2 tens in each      2 rows, 6 ones in each
$2 \times 100 = 200$      $2 \times 20 = 40$      $2 \times 6 = 12$

## ☆ Guided Practice

### Do You Understand?

1. Explain how an array shows multiplication.

### Do You Know How?

For **2–3**, complete each calculation.

2. $2 \times 24$      3. $3 \times 218$

## Independent Practice ☆

**Leveled Practice** For **4–5**, multiply. Complete each equation.

4. Find $3 \times 13$.

3 rows, 1 ten in each          3 rows, 3 ones in each

_____ × _____ = _____          _____ × _____ = _____

_____ + _____ = _____

5. Find $2 \times 105$

$$
\begin{array}{r}
105 \\
\times\ 2 \\
\hline
\end{array}
$$

_____  ⟵ 2 rows, 5 ones in each

+ _____  ⟵ 2 rows, 1 hundred in each
_____

**6. Model with Math** What multiplication equation do the place-value blocks show? Find the product. Then write a problem that could be solved using this model.

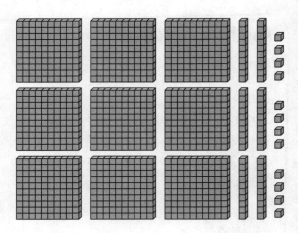

---

**7.** How many marbles are in 3 large bags and 4 small bags?

15 marbles     80 marbles

**8. Higher Order Thinking** How can the Distributive Property be used to find 4 × 875? Draw an array.

---

### ☑ Assessment Practice

**9.** Select all the expressions that have a value of 312.

☐ (3 × 100) + (3 × 4)
☐ 3 × 12
☐ 3 × 112
☐ (30 × 10) + (3 × 12)
☐ 3 × 104

**10.** Which are correct partial products for 54 × 9?

Ⓐ 36, 45
Ⓑ 36, 450
Ⓒ 540, 36
Ⓓ 32, 450

  

Name_____

Activity

★ ☆ ★
**Solve & Share**

Use only the numbers shown on the diagram and the operation symbols (+, −, ×, ÷) to determine the area of the unshaded rectangle below. **Solve this problem using any strategy you choose.**

Use structure and what you know about calculating area to solve this problem. *Show your work in the space below!*

**I can ...**
use area models and partial products to multiply.

**I can also** look for patterns to solve problems.

**Look Back!** **Use Structure** Are these equations equal? Explain.

$8 \times (10 - 4) = n$

$(8 \times 10) - (8 \times 4) = n$

**Essential Question** **How Can You Use an Area Model and Partial Products to Multiply?**

**A** A garden is in the shape of a rectangle. It is 8 feet wide and 25 feet long. What is the area of the garden?

A numerical expression contains numbers and at least one operation. 8 × 25 is a numerical expression.

**B** **What You Show**

25 ft

8 ft | 20 | 5

You can use a rectangular area model to show multiplication. The product of 8 × 25 is the area of the rectangle.

**C** **What You Think**

Estimate: 8 × 25 is about 8 × 30 = 240.

20      5

8 | 8 × 20 | 8 × 5

8 × 20 = 160    8 × 5 = 40

160 + 40 = 200

The Distributive Property says that multiplying a sum by a number is the same as multiplying each part of the sum by that number and adding the partial products.
8 × 25 = (8 × 20) + (8 × 5)

**D** **What You Record**

$$
\begin{array}{r}
25 \\
\times\ 8 \\
\hline
40 \\
+\ 160 \\
\hline
200
\end{array}
$$
  8 × 5 ones
  8 × 2 tens

The area of the garden is 200 square feet.

The product, 200, is close to the estimate of 240. The answer is reasonable.

**Convince Me!** **Use Structure** Does 12 − (4 × 2) = (12 − 4) × (12 − 2)? Explain.

Practice  Tools  Assessment

## Another Example!

Find $5 \times 123$.

```
       100          20  3
   5  [ 5 × 100 ]  [    ]←5 × 3
                      ↑
                   5 × 20
```

$5 \times 100 = 500$

$5 \times 20 = 100$

$5 \times 3 = 15$

```
      123
    ×   5
    ─────
       15    5 × 3
      100    5 × 20
    + 500    5 × 100
    ─────
      615
```

You can use what you know about multiplying 2-digit numbers to multiply 3-digit numbers.

## ☆ Guided Practice

### Do You Understand?

1. What numerical expression is shown by the area model below?

```
        200        60   5
    7  [         ][    ]/
```

### Do You Know How?

2. Multiply. Use the area model and partial products.

```
        500        60    560
    7  [         ][    ]  ×  7
```

## Independent Practice ☆

**Leveled Practice** For **3–6**, multiply. Use the area model and partial products.

3.
```
        30          4    34
    6  [         ][    ]  × 6
```

4.
```
        90          9    99
    2  [         ][    ]  × 2
```

5. $3 \times 185$
```
        100        80   5
    3  [         ][    ]/
```

6. $8 \times 440$
```
        400             40
    8  [              ][  ]
```

# Problem Solving

**7. Model with Math** Last year, Anthony's grandmother gave him 33 silver coins and 16 gold coins to start a coin collection. Now Anthony has six times as many coins in his collection. How many coins does Anthony have in his collection? Complete the bar diagram to show your work.

coins in all

| | | | | | coins now

| | coins to start

---

**8.** Wyatt said he used partial products to write $7 \times 870 = 5,600 + 49$. Explain Wyatt's error and use math to justify your explanation.

**9. Higher Order Thinking** Tod Mountain is a mountain peak near Tyler, Texas. A ranger hiked 607 feet to and from the peak, each way. The ranger hiked 3 times in the past four weeks. How far did the ranger hike on Tod Mountain over the past four weeks?

---

**10.** Wendy plans to bring beverages for the school picnic. She has 5 gallons of iced tea. Also, she will bring 2 gallons of lemonade for every 10 people. How many total gallons of lemonade and iced tea does Wendy need to bring for 40 people? Complete the table.

| Number of People | Gallons of Lemonade | Gallons of Iced Tea | Total Gallons |
|---|---|---|---|
| 10 | 2 | 5 | |
| 20 | | | |
| 30 | | | |
| 40 | | | |

---

**11.** What is the missing factor?

$6 \times ? = 264$

    Ⓐ  50

    Ⓑ  44

    Ⓒ  40

    Ⓓ  30

**12.** Which are the partial products for this area model?

$7 \times 228$

$7 \times 228$

    Ⓐ  1,400, 144, 56

    Ⓑ  14,000, 140, 56

    Ⓒ  56, 14, 1,400

    Ⓓ  56, 140, 1,400

Name _____

☆ ☆
**Solve & Share**

The horseshoe-pit model below has an area of 228 square feet. The length of one part of the pit was erased by mistake. What is the length of the missing section, *x*? **Solve any way you choose.** Explain how you found the answer.

**I can ...**
use area models and partial products to multiply.

**I can also** use a math tool to help solve problems.

```
          30 ft              x
       ┌────────────────┬──────┐
6 ft   │                │      │
       └────────────────┴──────┘
```

You can use appropriate tools. How can you use place-value blocks or drawings to solve this problem? *Show your work in the space above!*

**Look Back!** What multiplication equation can be used to represent the horseshoe-pit model above?

**Essential Question** **How Do You Multiply with Greater Numbers?**

**A**

The Rails-to-Trails Preservation opened a new section of a biking trail. The section is 6 yards wide. What is its area? Calculate 6 × 1,842.

The process for multiplying is the same regardless of the number of digits.

Trail Length: 1,842 yards

**B** Find 6 × 1,842 using an area model and partial products.

Estimate: 6 × 1,842 is about 6 × 2,000 = 12,000.

|  | 1,000 | 800 | 40 | 2 |
|---|---|---|---|---|
| 6 | 6 × 1,000 | 6 × 800 | 6 × 40 | 6 × 2 |

The area of 11,052 is reasonable because it is close to the estimate of 12,000.

**C** Remember you can find partial products in any order.

$$\begin{array}{r} 1,842 \\ \times\ \ \ 6 \\ \hline 12 \\ 240 \\ 4,800 \\ +\ 6,000 \\ \hline 11,052 \end{array}$$

6 × 2
6 × 40
6 × 800
6 × 1,000

The new section is 11,052 square yards.

**Convince Me!** **Use Structure** How is the process of using partial products to find the final product the same for each of these calculations? How is it different? Explain.

$$\begin{array}{r} 34 \\ \times\ 5 \\ \hline \end{array} \qquad \begin{array}{r} 234 \\ \times\ 5 \\ \hline \end{array} \qquad \begin{array}{r} 1,234 \\ \times\ \ \ 5 \\ \hline \end{array}$$

Name_____

# ☆ Guided Practice

## Do You Understand?

**1.** What multiplication expression is shown by the area model below?

|  | 1,000 | 400 | 5 |
| 4 |

## Do You Know How?

For **2**, multiply. Use the area model and partial products.

**2.** 5 × 1,117

|  | 1,000 | 100 | 7 |
| 5 |
|  |  | 10 |

$$\begin{array}{r} 1{,}117 \\ \times \quad 5 \\ \hline \end{array}$$

Use an estimate to check if your answer is reasonable.

# Independent Practice ☆

For **3–8**, multiply. Use the area model and partial products.

**3.**

|  | 1,000 | 90 | 2 |
| 8 |

$$\begin{array}{r} 1{,}092 \\ \times \quad 8 \\ \hline \end{array}$$

**4.**

|  | 4,000 | 200 | 1 |
| 3 |
|  |  | 60 |

$$\begin{array}{r} 4{,}261 \\ \times \quad 3 \\ \hline \end{array}$$

**5.**

|  | 1,000 | 900 | 90 |
| 2 |

$$\begin{array}{r} 1{,}990 \\ \times \quad 2 \\ \hline \end{array}$$

**6.**

|  | 2,000 | 300 | 7 |
| 6 |
|  |  | 40 |

$$\begin{array}{r} 2{,}347 \\ \times \quad 6 \\ \hline \end{array}$$

**7.**

|  | 3,000 | 2 |
| 5 |
|  | 20 |

$$\begin{array}{r} 3{,}022 \\ \times \quad 5 \\ \hline \end{array}$$

**8.**

|  | 1,000 | 900 | 9 |
| 7 |
|  |  | 90 |

$$\begin{array}{r} 1{,}999 \\ \times \quad 7 \\ \hline \end{array}$$

# Problem Solving

9. **Be Precise** There are usually 365 days in each year. Every fourth year is called a leap year and has one extra day in February. How many days are there in 8 years if 2 of the years are leap years?

10. There are 1,250 seeds in each package. There are 5 packages. How many seeds are there in all?

11. A cat breeder has 6 Sphynx kittens and 7 Persian kittens for sale. If all 13 kittens sell, how much money will the breeder earn? Write and solve equations. Tell what your variables represent.

KITTENS

Sphynx $775

Persian $698

FOR SALE

12. **Higher Order Thinking** Patricia creates a design using 1,025 tiles. She doubles the number of tiles to make a second design. Her third design uses 3 times as many tiles as the second design. How many tiles does Patricia use in her third design? Explain.

13. Which are the correct partial products of 3 × 3,672?

  Ⓐ 6; 21; 1,800; 9,000
  Ⓑ 9,000; 1,800; 210; 6
  Ⓒ 210; 1,800; 9,000
  Ⓓ 6; 210; 180; 9,000

14. Select all the expressions that have 1,600 as a partial product.

  ☐ 4 × 4,381
  ☐ 8 × 3,240
  ☐ 4 × 1,408
  ☐ 2 × 7,881
  ☐ 8 × 2,021

Name_____

Determine the products for the expressions given below. Use mental math to solve. Explain your thinking. **Solve these problems using any strategy you choose.**

**I can ...**
use mental math strategies based on place value and properties of operations to multiply.

**I can also** look for patterns to solve problems.

You can use structure to multiply the numbers in any order and make the computations easier. *Show your work in the space below!*

25 × 9 × 4

50 × 5 × 2

2 × 8 × 25

**Look Back!** Describe two different ways to find 4 × 97.

## Essential Question: How Can You Multiply Mentally?

**A**

Three cyclists rode their bikes the distances shown in the table. Use mental math to calculate the total distance Pam and Anna each rode.

You can use properties of operations to help multiply mentally. According to the Commutative Property of Multiplication, you can multiply in any order.

| DATA | Cyclist | Distance |
|---|---|---|
| | Pam | 325 miles a month for 4 months |
| | Anna | 25 miles a week for 8 weeks |
| | George | 398 miles a month for 3 months |

**B**

Multiply 4 × 325 to find the distance Pam rode.

To multiply mentally, you can break apart numbers using place value and the Distributive Property.

Think:
$$4 \times 325 = 4 \times 300 + 4 \times 25$$
$$= 1{,}200 + 100$$
$$= 1{,}300$$

Pam rode 1,300 miles.

**C**

Multiply 8 × 25 to find the distance Anna rode.

To multiply mentally, you can break apart and rearrange numbers using the Commutative and Associative Properties.

Think:
$$8 \times 25 = (4 \times 2) \times 25$$
$$= 2 \times (4 \times 25)$$
$$= 2 \times 100$$
$$= 200$$

Anna rode 200 miles.

**Convince Me!** **Use Structure** In the work for 4 × 325 above, why was 25 not broken into 20 and 5? Explain.

Practice   Tools   Assessment

## Another Example!

Determine the distance George rode.

Find $3 \times 398$. 400 is close to 398.
Find $3 \times 400$ and adjust the answer.

$3 \times 400 = 1,200$
$398 + 2 = 400$ $\qquad 3 \times 2 = 6$

Adjust the answer by subtracting 6.
$1,200 - 6 = 1,194$

George rode 1,194 miles in 3 months.

You can use compensation to multiply mentally. Choose numbers close to the numbers in the problem and then adjust the answer.

## ☆ Guided Practice

### Do You Understand?

1. Why was 6 subtracted from 1,200 in the problem above?

### Do You Know How?

For **2**, multiply mentally to find the product. Explain which strategy you used.

2. $8 \times 903$?

# Independent Practice ☆

**Leveled Practice** For **3–10**, multiply mentally to find each product. Explain which strategy you used.

3. $6 \times 250 = (3 \times$ _____$) \times 250$

4. $4 \times 506 = 4 \times ($_____$ + $_____$)$

5. $4 \times 1,995$

6. $22 \times 5$

7. $404 \times 6$

8. $7 \times 250$

9. $2 \times 395$

10. $9 \times 56$

# Problem Solving

**11.** Each elephant at a zoo eats 100 pounds of hay and 5 pounds of fruits and vegetables every day. How many pounds of food does the zoo need to feed one elephant for one week? Use mental math to solve.

There are 7 days in 1 week.

**12.** Ashley and 3 friends are planning a trip. The cost of the trip is $599 per person. How much will the trip cost Ashley and her friends? Explain the mental math strategy you used to find the answer.

**13.** Kyle has a rock collection. On Monday, he found 16 new rocks. On Tuesday, he gave 9 rocks to his friends. After giving away the rocks, Kyle had 122 rocks left in his collection. How many rocks did Kyle have to start with?

**14. Critique Reasoning** Quinn used compensation to find the product of $4 \times 307$. First, she found $4 \times 300 = 1,200$. Then she adjusted the product by subtracting 4 groups of 7 to get her final answer of 1,172. Explain Quinn's mistake and find the correct answer.

**15. Higher Order Thinking** Do you think it would be better to use breaking apart and the Distributive Property or compensation to find the product of $5 \times 328$? Explain why and show how to find the product.

## ☑ Assessment Practice

**16.** Select all of the expressions that show how to use mental math to find the product of $4 \times 27$.

- ☐ $(4 \times 20) + (4 \times 7)$
- ☐ $4 \times (20 \times 7)$
- ☐ $(4 \times 30) - (4 \times 3)$
- ☐ $(4 \times 25) + (4 \times 2)$
- ☐ $4 \times 2 \times 7$

Some mental math strategies include both compensation and properties of operations.

Name _____

Activity

**Solve & Share**

A cineplex has 4 movie theaters. Each theater has 342 floor seats and 85 mezzanine seats. How many people can the cineplex seat? *Solve this problem using any strategy you choose*. Explain your solution.

**I can ...**
choose an appropriate strategy to multiply.

**I can also** be precise in my work.

You can be precise and use the information given to calculate accurately. *Show your work in the space above!*

**Look Back!** What strategy or strategies did you use to solve this problem? Explain why.

**Essential Question** **What Strategy Will You Use to Multiply?**

**A**

*Paying for pothole damage to cars can be costly. The table shows the cost of some car repairs. What is the total cost of the repairs?*

Think about the numbers you need to multiply to help you choose a strategy.

### Repairs Due to Pothole Damage

| Item | Cost | Amount Purchased |
|------|------|------------------|
| Tires | $125 each | 4 |
| Paint | $1,450 per coat | 2 |

**B** Find the cost for the tires, c.

$4 \times \$125 = c$

Estimate: $4 \times 125$ is about $4 \times 120 = 480$.

Break apart 125 using place value and the Distributive Property.

$$4 \times 125 = 4 \times (100 + 25)$$
$$= 4 \times 100 + 4 \times 25$$
$$= 400 + 100$$
$$= 500$$

$c = 500$

The tire repairs cost $500.

**C** Find the cost of the paint, y. $2 \times \$1,450 = y$

Estimate: $2 \times 1,450$ is about $2 \times 1,500 = 3,000$.

Use an area model and partial products.

```
        1,000        400   50
   2  [          |        |  ]
```

```
    1,450
  ×     2
  ───────
      100    2 × 50
      800    2 × 400
  + 2,000    2 × 1,000
  ───────
    2,900
```

$y = 2,900$

To paint the car costs $2,900.

**D** Find the total cost of the repairs, z.

$\$500 + \$2,900 = z$

Estimate: $500 + 2,900$ is about $500 + 3,000 = 3,500$.

Use compensation to add.

$500 + 3,000 = 3,500$
3,000 is 100 more than 2,900.
Subtract 100.
$3,500 - 100 = 3,400$

$z = 3,400$

The total cost of the repairs was $3,400.

**Convince Me!** **Reasoning** Explain why the answers to each part of the problem above are reasonable.

Name _____

# ☆ Guided Practice

## Do You Understand?

**1.** A tire shop sells 3 tires that cost $175 each, which includes a fourth tire for free. Is this more or less expensive than buying 4 tires that cost $135 each?

## Do You Know How?

For **2–5**, find each product by choosing an appropriate strategy.

**2.**   74
   × 6

**3.**    819
   ×   5

**4.** 4 × 309

**5.** 3 × 354

# Independent Practice ☆

For **6–21**, find each product by choosing an appropriate strategy.

**6.**   25
   × 6

**7.**   83
   × 5

**8.**   62
   × 4

**9.**   89
   × 7

**10.**   245
   ×   3

**11.**   318
   ×   9

**12.**   103
   ×   5

**13.**   314
   ×   8

**14.** 4 × 4,347

**15.** 6 × 2,716

**16.** 7 × 1,287

**17.** 3 × 1,942

**18.** 2,319 × 5

**19.** 1,467 × 5

**20.** 6,006 × 9

**21.** 9,749 × 5

# Problem Solving

**22. Make Sense and Persevere** Maura's dance team wants to buy costumes that cost $56 each. They have $523 saved in a fund. How much money will they have left in the fund after they buy 9 costumes?

What is the hidden question you have to answer first?

**23.** Elaine rents a car for 5 days. It costs $44 each day to rent the car and $7 each day for insurance. At the end of the trip she spends $35 to fill the car with gas. What is the total cost for Elaine to use the car?

**24.** At the Math Club ceremony, there were 17 tables with 8 people seated at each table. Each guest received 2 certificates. How many certificates were distributed at the ceremony?

**25.** Water erupting from geysers can reach a temperature of 244°F. The average temperature in Yellowstone National Park is 35°F. Calculate the difference between these two temperatures.

**26. Higher Order Thinking** On Monday, Paolo sold 21 tickets to the dance. On Tuesday, he sold three times as many tickets as he sold on Monday. On Wednesday, he sold twice as many tickets as he sold on Tuesday. How many total tickets did Paolo sell in the three days?

## ✅ Assessment Practice

**27.** Mr. Tran would like to buy a new sofa that costs $934. He can pay the total all at once, or he can make a $125 payment each month for 8 months. How much less does it cost to pay all at once? Write equations to show how you solve. Tell what your variables represent.

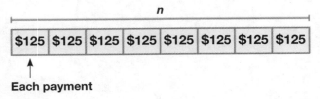

*n*

| $125 | $125 | $125 | $125 | $125 | $125 | $125 | $125 |

↑
**Each payment**

Name_____

**Solve & Share**

Kevin took 120 color photos and 128 black and white photos on a field trip. Marco took 2 times as many photos as Kevin. How many photos did Marco take? *Solve this problem using any strategy you choose. Use the bar diagram to help.*

Kevin

Marco

**I can ...**

apply the math I know to solve problems.

**I can also** solve multi-step problems.

### Thinking Habits

*Be a good thinker! These questions can help you.*

- How can I use math I know to solve this problem?

- How can I use pictures, objects, or an equation to represent the problem?

- How can I use numbers, words, and symbols to solve the problem?

**Look Back!** **Model with Math** What representation did you use to solve the problem and show relationships?

**Essential Question** How Can You Represent a Situation with a Math Model?

**A**

*An art show uses 9 teams of art judges. If each team judges the work of 13 painters and 14 sculptors, how many artists attend the show?*

### What do you need to find?

I need to find how many artists each team judges.

I need to find the total number of artists.

Each team judges 27 artists.

**B** ### How can I model with math?

**I can**

- use bar diagrams and equations to represent and solve this problem.

- decide if my results make sense.

**C** Find $9 \times 27$.

Here's my thinking.

Use a bar diagram. Write and solve an equation.

*a* artists

| 27 | 27 | 27 | 27 | 27 | 27 | 27 | 27 | 27 |

↑
number of artists for each team of judges

$a = 9 \times 27$

$a = 243$

There are 243 artists at the show.

**Convince Me!** **Model with Math** How could you decide if your answer makes sense?

# Guided Practice

**Model with Math**

Sharon's Stationery Store contains 1,219 boxes of cards. May's Market contains 3 times as many boxes of cards. How many boxes, *b*, does May's Market contain?

> When you model with math, you can draw a bar diagram and write an equation to represent the relationships in the problem.

1. Explain how to use a picture to represent the problem and show relationships.

2. What equation can you write to represent the problem?

3. What is the solution to the problem?

# Independent Practice

**Model with Math**

Annie has 6 albums of stamps in her stamp collection. Each album contains 440 stamps. How many stamps, *s*, does Annie have in her collection? Use Exercises 4–6 to answer the question.

4. Draw a picture and write an equation to represent the problem.

5. What previously learned math can you use to solve the problem?

6. What is the solution to the problem? Explain why your solution makes sense.

# Problem Solving

**Hauling Fuel**

A truck like the one shown delivers a load of gasoline to a gas station 3 times a week. The storage tank at the gas station holds 9 loads of fuel. How much more gas does the storage tank hold than the truck?

Hauls 2,700 gallons

7. **Make Sense and Persevere** What do you know and what do you need to determine?

When you model with math, you use math to represent real-world situations.

8. **Make Sense and Persevere** What do you need to know to determine how much more the tank holds than the truck?

9. **Model with Math** Explain how to use bar diagrams and equations to represent the problem and solve.

Shade a path from **START** to **FINISH**.
Follow the differences that are correct.
You can only move up, down, right,
or left.

**I can ...**
subtract multi-digit whole
numbers.

**I can also** be precise in my work.

| **Start** | | | | |
|---|---|---|---|---|
| 812<br>− 44<br>**768** | 929<br>− 879<br>**150** | 511<br>− 423<br>**112** | 767<br>− 31<br>**636** | 698<br>− 12<br>**586** |
| 621<br>− 85<br>**536** | 341<br>− 299<br>**142** | 486<br>− 230<br>**256** | 825<br>− 789<br>**36** | 333<br>− 111<br>**222** |
| 543<br>− 97<br>**446** | 836<br>− 788<br>**48** | 178<br>− 98<br>**80** | 123<br>− 53<br>**30** | 342<br>− 88<br>**254** |
| 111<br>− 87<br>**76** | 876<br>− 55<br>**72** | 912<br>− 842<br>**170** | 282<br>− 32<br>**150** | 293<br>− 95<br>**198** |
| 684<br>− 485<br>**299** | 922<br>− 87<br>**865** | 312<br>− 219<br>**193** | 986<br>− 887<br>**199** | 876<br>− 543<br>**333** |

**Finish**

# Vocabulary Review

**A-Z**
Glossary

## Word List

- array
- Associative Property of Multiplication
- Commutative Property of Multiplication
- compensation
- Distributive Property
- estimate
- numerical expression
- partial product

## Understand Vocabulary

**1.** Circle the property shown by $4 \times (6 + 2) = (4 \times 6) + (4 \times 2)$.

   Associative        Commutative        Distributive

**2.** Circle the property shown by $2 \times 134 = 134 \times 2$.

   Associative        Commutative        Distributive

**3.** Circle the property shown by $(1 \times 3) \times 7 = 1 \times (3 \times 7)$.

   Associative        Commutative        Distributive

**4.** Draw a line from each vocabulary word to its example.

array

compensation

estimate

numerical expression

partial products

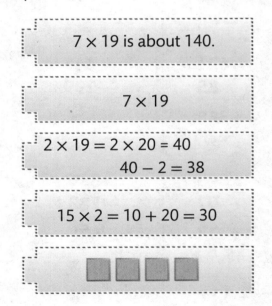

$7 \times 19$ is about 140.

$7 \times 19$

$2 \times 19 = 2 \times 20 = 40$
$40 - 2 = 38$

$15 \times 2 = 10 + 20 = 30$

## Use Vocabulary in Writing

**5.** Find $4 \times 114$. Use at least three terms from the Word List to describe how to find the product.

Name_____

**Set A** | pages 81–84 _____

Use basic facts, place value, and multiplication properties to multiply by multiples of 10 and 100.

Find 4 × 60.

4 × 60 = 4 × 6 tens
4 × 60 = (4 × 6) tens
4 × 60 = 24 × 10
4 × 60 = 240

Find 4 × 600.

4 × 600 = 4 × 6 hundreds
4 × 600 = (4 × 6) hundreds
4 × 600 = 24 × 100
4 × 600 = 2,400

Find 4 × 6,000.

4 × 6,000 = 4 × 6 thousands
4 × 6,000 = (4 × 6) thousands
4 × 6,000 = 24 × 1,000
4 × 6,000 = 24,000

**Remember** when the product of a basic fact ends in zero, the answer will have an extra zero.

**Reteaching**

**1.** 8 × 60          **2.** 3 × 10

**3.** 6 × 50          **4.** 5 × 300

**5.** 7,000 × 4       **6.** 2 × 900

**7.** 80 × 8          **8.** 400 × 5

**9.** 30 × 9          **10.** 5 × 8,000

**11.** 700 × 8        **12.** 9,000 × 6

**13.** 7 × 9,000      **14.** 5 × 100

**15.** 20 × 5         **16.** 5 × 4,000

**17.** 5 × 500        **18.** 3 × 2,000

**Set B** | pages 85–88 _____

Use rounding to estimate 9 × 1,993.

Round 1,993 to 2,000.

9 × 1,993
↓
9 × 2,000 = 18,000

So, 9 × 1,993 is about 18,000.

**Remember** to round a three-digit number to the nearest hundred and a four-digit number to the nearest thousand.

Estimate each product.

**1.** 8 × 7,632       **2.** 493 × 3

**3.** 9,379 × 5       **4.** 678 × 6

**5.** 707 × 4         **6.** 5,703 × 3

**7.** 483 × 6         **8.** 6 × 8,166

Use an array and partial products to find
3 × 121.

3 × 100 = 300

3 × 20 = 60

3 × 1 = 3

300 + 60 + 3 = 363

**Remember** to line up the partial products carefully.

1.    75
   × 5

2.    253
   ×    4

3.    214
   ×    7

4.    1,341
   ×    7

Use the Distributive Property to find 5 × 45.

Use place value to break apart 45 as 40 + 5.

```
        40          5
5 [              |    ]
```

Use the Distributive Property:

5 × 45 = 5 × (40 + 5)
$\quad$ = (5 × 40) + (5 × 5)
$\quad$ = 200 + 25
$\quad$ = 225

So, 5 × 45 = 225.

**Remember** that you can use the Distributive Property to help multiply larger numbers.

1. 7 × 45

2. 326 × 9

3. 720 × 6

4. 3 × 46

5. 371 × 8

6. 5 × 95

7. 88 × 3

8. 4 × 1,865

9. 57 × 3

10. 209 × 7

**Set E** pages 97–100

All your strategies may be used to find larger products.

Use the Distributive Property to find 3 × 1,275.

Use expanded notation and place value to construct an area model.

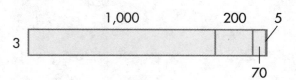

$$3 \times 1{,}275 = 3 \times (1{,}000 + 200 + 70 + 5)$$
$$= (3 \times 1{,}000) + (3 \times 200) +$$
$$(3 \times 70) + (3 \times 5)$$
$$= 3{,}000 + 600 + 210 + 15$$
$$= 3{,}825$$

**Remember** to estimate to check that your answer is reasonable.

**1.** 1,468 × 4     **2.** 361 × 3

**3.** 25 × 7     **4.** 2,189 × 7

**5.** 6 × 987     **6.** 8 × 22

**7.** 763 × 5     **8.** 14 × 9

**9.** 171 × 8     **10.** 22 × 9

**11.** 1,409 × 5     **12.** 17 × 6

**Set F** pages 101–104

You can use properties of operations or compensation to multiply mentally.

Use the Commutative and Associative Properties to find 8 × 50.

$$8 \times 50 = (2 \times 4) \times 50$$
$$= (4 \times 2) \times 50$$
$$= 4 \times (2 \times 50)$$
$$= 4 \times 100$$
$$= 400$$

Use compensation to find 9 × 67.
Think: 67 = 70 − 3
Multiply mentally 9 × 70.
9 × 70 = 630
Adjust by subtracting
9 × 3, or 27.
Subtract: 630 − 27 = 603
So, 9 × 67 = 603.

**Remember** that you can use diagrams or properties of operations to help multiply mentally.

**1.** 18 × 2     **2.** 48 × 5

**3.** 52 × 7     **4.** 33 × 6

**5.** 97 × 7     **6.** 88 × 4

**7.** 239 × 4     **8.** 148 × 5

**9.** 233 × 6     **10.** 937 × 7

You can use the strategy that fits the problem best. You know place-value strategies, the Distributive Property, area models, and compensation.

Place value:
$8 \times 359 = 8 \times 3$ hundreds $+ 8 \times 5$ tens $+ 8 \times 9$ ones

The Distributive Property:
$7 \times 4,056 = 7 \times (4,000 + 50 + 6)$
$\qquad\qquad = (7 \times 4,000) + (7 \times 50) + (7 \times 6)$

Compensation:
$6 \times 495$
$(6 \times 500) - (6 \times 5)$

**Remember** to use an estimate to check if your answer is reasonable.

1.  $\begin{array}{r} 43 \\ \times\ 8 \\ \hline \end{array}$
2.  $\begin{array}{r} 57 \\ \times\ 9 \\ \hline \end{array}$

3.  $\begin{array}{r} 215 \\ \times\ \ 7 \\ \hline \end{array}$
4.  $\begin{array}{r} 869 \\ \times\ \ 2 \\ \hline \end{array}$

5.  $\begin{array}{r} 4,233 \\ \times\ \ \ \ 7 \\ \hline \end{array}$
6.  $\begin{array}{r} 3,261 \\ \times\ \ \ \ 4 \\ \hline \end{array}$

7.  $\begin{array}{r} 1,250 \\ \times\ \ \ \ 8 \\ \hline \end{array}$
8.  $\begin{array}{r} 2,239 \\ \times\ \ \ \ 5 \\ \hline \end{array}$

Think about these questions to help you **model with math**.

### Thinking Habits

- How can I use math I know to help solve this problem?

- How can I use pictures, objects, or an equation to represent the problem?

- How can I use numbers, words, and symbols to solve the problem?

**Remember** that a bar diagram can help you write an equation.

Mia has a collection of 34 dolls. A toy store's warehouse has 5 times as many dolls.

1.  Use pictures, a bar diagram, or an equation to find the number of dolls in the warehouse.

2.  How can you decide if your answer is reasonable?

Name_____

**1.** Use numbers from the box to show how to multiply 126 by 3.

$$
\begin{array}{r}
126 \\
\times\quad 3 \\
\hline
\Box \\
\Box \\
+\ \Box \\
\hline
\Box
\end{array}
$$

| 18 | 30 |
|----|-----|
| 60 | 180 |
| 600 | 300 |
| 378 | 387 |

**2.** Alberto rode the train 198 miles round trip 4 times last month. Explain how to use mental math to find the total distance Alberto traveled.

**3.** Mr. Ortiz sells tortillas in bags of 25 and in bags of 50. If he sells 4 bags of 50 and 6 bags of 25, how many tortillas did Mr. Ortiz sell?

Ⓐ  10 tortillas      Ⓒ  350 tortillas

Ⓑ  170 tortillas     Ⓓ  3,500 tortillas

**4. A.** What are the partial products when finding $1{,}874 \times 3$? Select all that apply.

☐ 5,400        ☐ 2,000

☐ 3,000        ☐ 210

☐ 2,400        ☐ 12

**B.** Find the product of 1,874 and 3.

**5.** A science class is growing some fruit and vegetable plants on a plot of land behind their school. Each section is laid out in rows.

| DATA | Produce | Number of Rows |
|------|---------|----------------|
| | Strawberries | 65 |
| | Peppers | 18 |
| | Squash | 11 |
| | Tomatoes | 22 |

**A.** There are 9 strawberry plants planted in each row. Write and solve an equation to find how many strawberry plants were planted.

**B.** There are 9 pepper plants planted in each row. Draw an area model and show the partial products to find how many pepper plants are planted behind the school.

**6.** Select all the expressions that could be used to find 1,235 × 9.

- ☐ 9 × (1,000 + 200 + 20 + 5)
- ☐ 9 × (1,000 + 200 + 30 + 5)
- ☐ (9 × 1,000) + (9 × 200) + (9 × 30) + (9 × 5)
- ☐ 9 × 1,235
- ☐ 1,235 + 9

---

**7.** Draw a model to find 365 × 3.



365 × 3 = _____

---

**8.** Select all of the expressions that have a product of 640.

- ☐ (6 × 100) + (4 × 10)
- ☐ 9 × 54
- ☐ 60 × 4 × 1
- ☐ 160 × 4
- ☐ (6 × 100) × (4 × 10)

**9.** The table shows the number of hot drinks sold in a busy coffee shop in 1 week.

| Type | Number |
|------|--------|
| Coffee | 835 |
| Latte | 567 |
| Mocha | 200 |
| Cappuccino | 139 |

DATA

**A.** If the same number of cups of coffee were sold for 6 weeks in a row, how many cups would be sold in all?



**B.** The special drink of the month was an iced mocha. The shop sold 5 times as many iced mochas in one week as hot mochas. How many more iced mochas were sold than hot mochas in 4 weeks? Explain.

**10.** Tickets for a resort cost $1,182 each for adults and $459 each for children. Find the cost for 3 adult tickets and 3 child tickets. Explain how you know your answer is reasonable.

**11.** Which expression has the same value as 5 × 617?

Ⓐ (5 × 6) + (5 × 1) + (5 × 7)

Ⓑ (5 × 60) + (5 × 10) + (5 × 70)

Ⓒ (5 × 600) + (5 × 1) + (5 × 7)

Ⓓ (5 × 600) + (5 × 10) + (5 × 7)

**12.** Which of the following is equivalent to (400 × 3) + (36 × 3)?

Ⓐ 436 ÷ 3

Ⓑ 400 × 10

Ⓒ 436 × 3

Ⓓ 400 × 3 + 36

**13.** Find 3 × 312. Draw a bar diagram to solve.

**14.** Bea's Bakery bakes 215 cookies and 45 muffins every hour. How many baked goods are baked in 4 hours?

**15.** Write and solve an equation that represents the given bar diagram.

| b | | | |
|---|---|---|---|
| 48 | 48 | 48 | 48 |

**16.** Which of the following is equivalent to 8 × 493? Select all that apply.

☐ (8 × 400) + (8 × 90) + (8 × 3)

☐ (8 × 400) + 93

☐ 493 × 8

☐ (8 × 500) − (8 × 93)

☐ (8 × 500) − (8 × 7)

**17.** Mr. Luca would like to purchase a digital keyboard for each of his 3 nieces and 1 nephew. The keyboard costs $105.

**A.** Mr. Luca thinks the total cost should be about $200. Is this amount reasonable? Explain.

**B.** Write and solve an equation to find the total cost of the keyboards. Explain why your answer is reasonable.

**18.** What is the product of 5 × 1,903?

Ⓐ 9,515

Ⓑ 9,505

Ⓒ 9,155

Ⓓ 965

**19.** How can you use mental math to find the product of 6 × 295?

**20. A.** Select all the partial products for 8 × 321.

☐ 8

☐ 80

☐ 160

☐ 1,600

☐ 2,400

**B.** Find the product for **Part A** using the partial products.

Name_____

## Buying Classroom Computers

Jorge's school can purchase computers and printers for the prices shown. Information about the fourth-grade classes are given in the table.

Performance Task

| Fourth Grade Classes | | |
|---|---|---|
| Teacher | Money Raised | Number of Students |
| Mr. Jones | $6,000 | 25 |
| Ms. Sanchez | $9,000 | 24 |
| Ms. Katz | $7,500 | 26 |

DATA

Desktop computer: $1,050

Laptop computer: $798

Printer: $128

1. Jorge's teacher is Ms. Sanchez. His class wants to buy 8 desktop computers and 3 printers.

### Part A

What is the total cost of 8 desktop computers? Use place-value strategies and properties of operations.

### Part B

What is the total cost of 3 printers? Draw an array and show the partial products to find the cost.

### Part C

Did Jorge's class raise enough money to buy 8 computers and 3 printers? Explain.

**2.** Rachel's teacher is Mr. Jones. Her class wants to buy 7 computers and 2 printers.

**Part A**

How much more do 7 desktop computers cost than 7 laptop computers? Use bar diagrams and equations to represent and solve the problem.

**Part B**

What is another way to find the difference in the cost of 7 desktop computers and 7 laptop computers? Explain.

**3.** Miranda's teacher is Ms. Katz. Her class wants to buy 9 laptop computers and 4 printers. Miranda said the total cost should be $7,494. Is this amount reasonable? Explain. Does the class have enough money?

# Use Strategies and Properties to Multiply by 2-Digit Numbers

**Essential Questions:** How can you use a model to multiply?
How can you use the Distributive Property to multiply?
How can you use multiplication to solve problems?

**Digital Resources**

Interactive Student Edition   Activity   Visual Learning   Video   Practice

Assessment   Games   Tools   Glossary

Renewable energy comes from natural resources that never run out.

These huge turbines harness wind energy to produce electric power and reduce pollution caused by fossil fuels.

Let me get my kite! Here is a project on energy and multiplication.

**enVision STEM Project: Renewable Energy and Multiplication**

**Do Research** Use the Internet or other sources to find information about different sources of renewable energy.

**Journal: Write a Report** Include what you found. Also in your report:

- A wind farm is an area of land with a large number of turbines. Draw an array with 15 rows to show the turbines in a wind farm. How many turbines are in your wind farm?

- Some turbines produce 63 megawatt-hours of energy every week. Find how much energy one of these turbines would produce in one year. Remember, one year is 52 weeks.

# Review What You Know

## A-Z Vocabulary

Choose the best term from the box.
Write it on the blank.

- algorithm
- product
- array
- variable

**1.** You multiply numbers to find a(n) _____.

**2.** A(n) _____ shows the number of objects in rows and columns.

**3.** A symbol or letter that stands for a number is called a(n) _____.

## Multiplication

Find each product.

**4.** $4 \times 8$

**5.** $2 \times 9$

**6.** $9 \times 5$

**7.** $6 \times 8$

**8.** $16 \times 4$

**9.** $6 \times 68$

**10.** $87 \times 5$

**11.** $19 \times 9$

**12.** $128 \times 6$

## Rounding

Round each number to the nearest hundred.

**13.** 164

**14.** 8,263

**15.** 527

**16.** 2,498

**17.** 7,892

**18.** 472

You will use rounding to estimate products in this topic.

Round each number to the nearest thousand.

**19.** 8,685

**20.** 4,991

**21.** 62,549

**22.** 167,241

**23.** 77,268

**24.** 34,162

**25.** 1,372

**26.** 9,009

**27.** 121,619

**28. Construct Arguments** Explain how to round 608,149 to the nearest thousands place.

**PROJECT
4A**

## How high would a stack of sabal palms be?

**Project:** Explain the Processes

**PROJECT
4B**

## Can you estimate the weight of dozens of birds?

**Project:** Write a Report About the Northern Mockingbird

**PROJECT 4C**

## How many soccer players start in the Women's World Cup ?

**Project:** Create an Array Poster

**PROJECT 4D**

## How much weight can shotputters throw ?

**Project:** Compare Shot Masses

Name _____

## Solve & Share

The principal of a school needs to order supplies for 20 new classrooms. Each classroom needs the following items: 20 desks, 30 chairs, and 40 pencils. How many of each item does the principal need to order? **Solve these problems using any strategy you choose.**

You can use structure. What basic facts can you use to help solve these problems? How are they related? *Show your work in the space below!*

**I can ...**
use place-value strategies or properties of operations to multiply by multiples of 10.

**I can also** look for patterns to solve problems.

**Look Back!** Look at the factors and products. What patterns do you notice?

Essential Question **How Can You Multiply by Multiples of 10?**

**A**

*The number of visitors of each age group for the Sunny Day Amusement Park are shown below. How many children visit the park in 30 days?*

 You can use place-value strategies or properties of operations to multiply by multiples of 10.

TICKET  Adults under 65: **60**

Adults 65 and over: **40**

Children: **80**

Number of visitors each day

---

**B** **One Way**

Find 30 × 80.

Use basic facts and place value.

30 × 80 = 3 tens × 8 tens
　　　　 = 24 hundreds
　　　　 = 2,400

2,400 children visit the park in 30 days.

 10 × 10 = 100

**C** **Another Way**

Find 30 × 80.

Break apart numbers.
Use the Commutative Property and the Associative Property of Multiplication.

30 × 80 = (3 × 10) × (8 × 10)
　　　　 = 3 × 8 × 10 × 10
　　　　 = (3 × 8) × (10 × 10)
　　　　 = 24 × 100
　　　　 = 2,400

2,400 children visit the park in 30 days.

---

 **Convince Me!** **Look for Relationships** Use place value or properties of operations to determine how many adults age 65 and older visit the park in 30 days.

---

## Another Example!

Use the properties of operations to find $50 \times 60$.

$$50 \times 60 = 5 \times 10 \times 6 \times 10$$
$$= (5 \times 6) \times (10 \times 10)$$
$$= 30 \times 100$$
$$= 3{,}000$$

If the product of the basic fact ends in zero, the product has one more zero than you see in the factors.

## ☆ Guided Practice

### Do You Understand?

**1.** Find $50 \times 20$. How many zeros are in the product? Explain.

**2.** How many adults under 65 visit the park in 30 days?

### Do You Know How?

For **3–8**, use basic facts and place-value or properties of operations to find each product.

**3.** $30 \times 10$          **4.** $50 \times 10$

**5.** $20 \times 10$          **6.** $60 \times 20$

**7.** $90 \times 40$          **8.** $80 \times 50$

## Independent Practice ☆

For **9–16**, use basic facts and place-value or properties of operations to find each product.

**9.** $20 \times 70$     **10.** $70 \times 90$     **11.** $40 \times 20$     **12.** $40 \times 30$

**13.** $70 \times 40$    **14.** $20 \times 30$     **15.** $60 \times 40$     **16.** $60 \times 90$

For **17–22**, find the missing factor.

**17.** $10 \times$ _____ $= 100$     **18.** _____ $\times 20 = 1{,}600$     **19.** _____ $\times 30 = 1{,}500$

**20.** $20 \times$ _____ $= 1{,}000$     **21.** _____ $\times 90 = 8{,}100$     **22.** $60 \times$ _____ $= 4{,}200$

# Problem Solving

**23.** **Reasoning** The product of two factors is 4,200. If one of the factors is 60, what is the other factor? Explain.

**24.** **Algebra** There are 30 players on each high school football team. Explain how you can find the total number of players if there are 40 teams. Write and solve an equation.

**25.** Bob uses 2 gallons of water while brushing his teeth. He uses 10 gallons of water to wash clothes. How many more cups of water did Bob use while washing his clothes than brushing his teeth?

There are 16 cups in 1 gallon.

**26.** James walked 30 minutes each day for 90 days. Show how you can use place value or properties to find how many minutes James walked.

**27.** **Higher Order Thinking** What is one example of a product that will have the same number of zeros in the factors and the product? What is one example of a product that will NOT have the same number of zeros in the factors as the product?

## Assessment Practice

**28.** Select all of the expressions that have a product of 1,600.

- ☐ 20 × 80
- ☐ 20 × 60
- ☐ 40 × 40
- ☐ 60 × 30
- ☐ 90 × 20

**29.** Which expression has 50 as the missing factor?

Ⓐ  20 × ? = 1,000

Ⓑ  50 × ? = 3,000

Ⓒ  30 × ? = 1,800

Ⓓ  10 × ? = 1,000

Name_____

Activity

Solve & Share

There are 10 teams in a baseball league. Each team has 25 players. How many players are in the league? *Solve this problem using any strategy you choose.*

**I can ...**
use models and properties of operations to help multiply.

**I can also** choose and use a math tool to solve problems.

You can use appropriate tools. Place-value blocks or grid paper can help you visualize the problem. *Show your work in the space above!*

**Look Back!** How many players are in the league if there are 30 teams?

Explain how you can use your answer above to help solve this problem.

**Essential Question**

# How Can You Use an Array or an Area Model to Multiply?

**A**

*Max's Moving Company has boxes for packing books. If each box holds 24 books, how many books would fit into 20 boxes?*

Making an array with place-value blocks or using an area model helps to visualize the partial products.

24 Books

**B** Use place-value blocks to make an array.

Find $20 \times 24 = b$.

$$\begin{array}{r} 400 \\ + \ 80 \\ \hline 480 \end{array}$$ Partial Products

$20 \times 24 = 480$

$b = 480$

$20 \times 20 = 400$   $20 \times 4 = 80$

480 books will fit into 20 boxes.

**C** Draw an area model.

Find $20 \times 24 = b$.

$20 \times 20 = 400$

$20 \times 4 = 80$

$$\begin{array}{r} 400 \\ + \ 80 \\ \hline 480 \end{array}$$ Partial Products

$20 \times 24 = 480$

$b = 480$

480 books will fit into 20 boxes.

**Convince Me!** **Reasoning** In the problem above, is the product, 480, reasonable? Explain.

Name _____

# ☆ Guided Practice

## Do You Understand?

**1.** Draw an area model to show 20 × 26. Then find the product.

## Do You Know How?

**2.** The place-value block array shows 10 × 16. Find the product.

☐☐☐ ←— 10 groups of 10

+ ☐☐ ←— 10 groups of 6

_____

☐☐☐ ←— Sum of the partial products

# Independent Practice ☆

**Leveled Practice** For **3–8**, use place-value blocks, area models, or arrays to find each product.

**3.** 10 × 22

☐☐☐ ←— 10 groups of 20

+ ☐☐ ←— 10 groups of 2

_____

☐☐☐ ←— Sum of the partial products

**4.** 10 × 13

You can use a sheet of grid paper to draw arrays or area models.

☐☐☐ ←— 10 groups of 10

+ ☐☐ ←— 10 groups of 3

_____

☐☐☐ ←— Sum of the partial products

**5.** 20 × 35

**6.** 20 × 41

**7.** 30 × 29

**8.** 40 × 37

# Problem Solving

9. **Algebra** In the first 3 months of the year, an electronics store sold 1,446 cameras. How many cameras did the store sell in March? Write and solve an equation.

| Camera Sales | |
|---|---|
| **Month** | **Number Sold** |
| January | 486 |
| February | 385 |

DATA

10. For every camera sold in February, the store donated $2 to a charity. How much did the store donate?

---

11. **Model with Math** During a basketball game, 75 cups of fruit punch were sold. Each cup holds 20 fluid ounces. How many total fluid ounces of fruit punch were sold?

**Fluid ounces per cup**

12. **Higher Order Thinking** Describe how to correct the partial product that is not correct in the worked problem below. What is the correct product?

$$
\begin{array}{r}
27 \\
\times\ 73 \\
\hline
1,400 \\
49 \\
60 \\
+\ \ \ 21 \\
\hline
1,530
\end{array}
$$

---

### ✅ Assessment Practice

13. Which is greater?

15 × 30 or 22 × 20
Show your thinking.

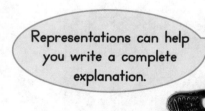

Representations can help you write a complete explanation.

Name_____

**Solve & Share**

Choose two factors from the numbers below to find a product that is as close to 1,600 as possible. *Solve this problem using any strategy you choose.*

| 24 | 32 | 61 | 78 |

**I can ...**
use rounding or compatible numbers to estimate.

**I can also** make math arguments.

What strategies do you know that can help you estimate a product? *Show your work in the space below!*

**Look Back!** **Construct Arguments** Why did you choose the two factors that you did? How do you know your factors will give the closest estimate of the product?

**Essential Question**

# What Strategies Can I Use When Estimating?

**A**

*The workers picked 14 dozen apples at Ms. Piper's apple grove and 12 dozen apples at Mr. Stuart's apple grove. There are 12 apples in one dozen. About how many apples did the workers pick?*

14 + 12 = 26 dozen
apples picked in total

1 dozen apples

There is more than one strategy you can use to estimate.

---

**B** ## One Way

Use rounding to estimate 26 × 12.

Round 26 to the nearest ten.
Round 12 to the nearest ten.

$$26 \times 12 = n$$
$$\downarrow \qquad \downarrow$$
$$30 \times 10 = 300$$

The workers picked about 300 apples.

Some problems do not need an exact answer.

**C** ## Another Way

Use compatible numbers to estimate 26 × 12.

Replace the factors with numbers that are close and easy to multiply.

26 is close to 25.      12 is close to 10.

$$25 \times 10 = n$$
$$250 = n$$

The workers picked about 250 apples.

---

**Convince Me! Reasoning** Sue said she could find an estimate for 26 × 12 by rounding only 1 factor and multiplying 26 × 10. Do you agree? Explain.

---

Practice  Tools  Assessment

# ☆Guided Practice

## Do You Understand?

**1.** In the example on the previous page, how do you know you only need an estimate and not an exact answer?

**2.** In the example on the previous page, what is another way you can multiply using compatible numbers by changing only one of the factors? Explain how you would find the estimated product.

## Do You Know How?

For **3–6**, estimate each product. Explain why you chose the strategy you used to estimate the product.

**3.** 24 × 18

**4.** 33 × 31

**5.** 38 × 22

**6.** 45 × 48

# Independent Practice ☆

For **7–12**, estimate each product. Explain why you chose the strategy you used to estimate the product.

**7.** 39 × 19

**8.** 28 × 27

**9.** 64 × 13

**10.** 42 × 17

**11.** 82 × 36

**12.** 54 × 18

For **13–14**, estimate to check if the given answer is reasonable.

**13.** 66 × 41 = 2,706

Rounds to _____ × _____ = _____

Reasonable      Not Reasonable

**14.** 34 × 52 = 2,288

Rounds to _____ × _____ = _____

Reasonable      Not Reasonable

Compare your estimate to the given answer to check if the answer is reasonable.

# Problem Solving

For **15–16**, use the table at the right.

**15.** About how many more Valencia orange trees than Temple orange trees does Mr. Gonzalez have? Explain.

**16.** About how many orange trees does Mr. Gonzalez have? Explain.

Your answer can be an estimate because an exact answer is not necessary.

**Mr. Gonzalez's Trees**

| Type of Orange Tree | Number of Rows | Number of Trees in Each Row |
|---|---|---|
| Hamlin | 28 | 38 |
| Temple | 38 | 28 |
| Valencia | 31 | 46 |

**17. Higher Order Thinking** How is using compatible numbers to estimate similar to using rounding? How is it different?

**18. Construct Arguments** Explain how you would use estimation to decide which has the greater product, 39 × 21 or 32 × 32.

## Assessment Practice

**19.** Select all of the expressions that could be used to estimate 32 × 14.

- ☐ 30 × 20
- ☐ 30 × 10
- ☐ 14 × 32
- ☐ 40 × 10
- ☐ 32 × 10

**20.** Select all of the equations that use compatible numbers to find an estimate for 28 × 24.

- ☐ 30 × 25 = 750
- ☐ 28 × 10 = 280
- ☐ 28 × 25 = 700
- ☐ 25 × 20 = 500
- ☐ 30 × 300 = 9,000

Name _____

## Lesson 4-4
### Arrays and Partial Products

**Solve & Share**

A theater contains 14 rows of seats with 23 seats in each row. How many seats are in the theater? *Solve this problem using any strategy you choose.*

**I can ...**
use place-value concepts and properties to multiply.

**I can also** model with math to solve problems.

You can use grid paper or arrays to show the problem. *Show your work in the space below!*

**Look Back!** **Use Structure** Theater seating is an example of objects that are arranged in rows and columns, or arrays. How do the number of rows and the number of seats in each row relate to the total number of seats?

**Essential Question**

# How Can You Multiply Using an Array?

**A**

*There are 13 toy dogs in each row of a carnival booth. Twenty rows contain toy bulldogs and 4 rows contain toy huskies. How many toy dogs are there?*

To solve this problem, you need to first find how many rows of toy dogs are in the booth.

    20 rows of toy bulldogs
  + 4 rows of toy huskies
—————————————————
    24 rows of toy dogs

There are 24 rows of toy dogs with 13 toy dogs in each row.

13 dogs per row

---

**B** Use an array to find $24 \times 13$.

$20 \times 10 = 200$

$4 \times 10 = 40$

$20 \times 3 = 60$

$4 \times 3 = 12$

Separate each factor into tens and ones.

Color each section a different color.

12, 40, 60, and 200 are partial products.

**C** Add the number of squares in each part of the array.

    12    $4 \times 3$ ones
    40    $4 \times 1$ ten
    60    $20 \times 3$ ones
 + 200   $20 \times 1$ ten
———————
  312

There are 312 toy dogs in the booth.

$24 \times 13 = 312$ is close to $25 \times 10 = 250$. The answer is reasonable.

---

**Convince Me! Model with Math** What 2-digit by 2-digit multiplication is shown by the model at the right? What is the product? Explain how you used the model to find the product.

---

  

## ☆ Guided Practice

### Do You Understand?

**1.** In the example on the previous page, what four simpler multiplication problems were used to find 24 × 13?

**2.** How can you use properties to help find the product of 24 × 13?

### Do You Know How?

For **3**, use the array drawn on a grid to find the product. Check if your answer is reasonable.

**3.**
$$\begin{array}{r} 24 \\ \times\ 16 \\ \hline \end{array}$$

## Independent Practice ☆

For **4–7**, use the array drawn on a grid to find each product.

**4.** 14 × 21

**5.** 14 × 12

Using the Commutative Property of Addition, you can add the partial products in any order.

**6.** 18 × 18

**7.** 15 × 13

# Problem Solving

**8.** Find the missing factor.
$20 \times ? = 420$
Explain how you solved.

**9.** The flagpole in front of City Hall in Lou's town is 35 feet tall. How many inches tall is the flagpole? Remember, there are 12 inches in 1 foot.

For **10–11**, use the array at the right.

**10. Model with Math** Maggie is making a balloon game for the school fair. Students throw darts to pop the balloons. Draw lines on the array to separate each factor into tens and ones. How many balloons are used to set up the game?

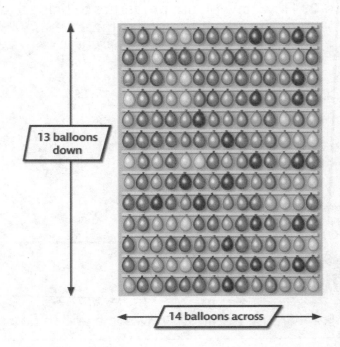

13 balloons down

14 balloons across

**11. Higher Order Thinking** Maggie knows she will have to completely refill the balloon board about 15 times. Write an equation to show the number of balloons Maggie will need.

## Assessment Practice

**12.** Insert the missing partial products. Then add to find the product.

> 200   60   6   1,200   120   30   12

$$\begin{array}{r} 13 \\ \times\ 23 \\ \hline 9 \\ \square \\ 60 \\ +\ \square \\ \hline \end{array}$$

$$\begin{array}{r} 33 \\ \times\ 42 \\ \hline 6 \\ \square \\ \square \\ +\ 1,200 \\ \hline \end{array}$$

**13.** Insert the missing factor in each equation.

> 49   53   79   15   47   25   28   84

$19 \times \square = 1,007$

$62 \times \square = 1,736$

$\square \times 37 = 1,813$

$15 \times \square = 1,260$

**Solve & Share**

A playground is divided into four sections as shown in the diagram below. Find the area of the playground. Explain how you found the answer. **Solve this problem using any strategy you choose.**

Activity

**I can ...**
use area models and properties of operations to multiply two 2-digit numbers.

**I can also** model with math to solve problems.

You can use drawings, area models, and properties of operations to model the math.

|  | 20 feet | 4 feet |
|---|---|---|
| 10 feet | | |
| 8 feet | | |

**Look Back!** Explain how you found the area of the blue part of the playground.

**Essential Question**

# How Can You Use the Distributive Property to Multiply?

**A**

There are 15 players on each baseball team of the Strike Out Club. How many players are on all of the teams in the Strike Out Club?

You can use an area model to show the Distributive Property.

There are 25 teams in the Strike Out Club.

---

**B** ## One Way

Use an area model and the Distributive Property to find 25 × 15.

Break apart 15 into 10 + 5.

25 × (10 + 5)
(25 × 10) + (25 × 5)

| 10 | 5 |

25 | 25 × 10 = 250 |

25 × 5 = 125

Add the partial products.

250
+ 125
375

---

**C** ## Another Way

Use an area model and the Distributive Property to find 25 × 15.

Break apart 25 into 20 + 5.

(20 + 5) × 15
(20 × 15) + (5 × 15)

| 15 |

20 | 20 × 15 = 300 |

5 | 5 × 15 = 75 |

Add the partial products.

300
+ 75
375

---

**D** ## Another Way

Use an area model and the Distributive Property to find 25 × 15.

Break apart both factors.

Break apart 25 into 20 + 5.
Break apart 15 into 10 + 5.

| 10 | 5 |

20 | 20 × 10 = 200 | 20 × 5 = 100 |

5 |

5 × 10 = 50    5 × 5 = 25

Add the partial products.

200
50
100
+ 25
375

---

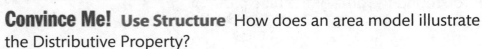

There are 375 players on the team.

---

**Convince Me!** **Use Structure** How does an area model illustrate the Distributive Property?

---

Practice  Tools  Assessment

# ☆ Guided Practice

## Do You Understand?

**1.** What four simpler multiplication problems are used to find 24 × 23?

**2.** How can an area model and the Distributive Property help you multiply? Use 12 × 16 to explain.

## Do You Know How?

**3.** Use the area model and the Distributive Property to find 35 × 12.

35 × 12 = _____

30 × 10 = _____

5 × 10 = _____

30 × 2 = _____

5 × 2 = _____

_____ + _____ + _____ + _____ = _____

# ☆ Independent Practice ☆

For **4–10**, draw an area model to find each product.

**4.** 18 × 25

**5.** 14 × 25

**6.** 22 × 88

**7.**  41
     × 12

**8.**  30
     × 27

**9.**  58
     × 19

**10.**  29
      × 50

# Problem Solving

**11.** Write 652,079 using number names and in expanded form.

**12. Number Sense** Sara estimated $23 \times 43$ using $20 \times 40$. Sam estimated $23 \times 43$ using $25 \times 40$. Will Sara's or Sam's method give an estimate closer to the exact answer? Explain.

**13. Use Structure** Each family of Florida Scrub Jays inhabits 25 acres of land. No other Scrub Jay families live within this area. How many acres of land are needed for 24 families of Florida Scrub Jays? Show how you can use the Distributive Property to solve this problem.

Inhabits 25 acres
of land

**14.** Marla wants to buy a new tablet that costs $565, including tax. She saved $15 per week for 30 weeks. Does Marla have enough money saved to buy the tablet? Explain.

**15. Higher Order Thinking** Which costs less: 13 oranges that cost 29 cents each or 17 apples that cost 25 cents each? How much less?

## ✓ Assessment Practice

**16.** Select all of the partial products which would be used to find $19 \times 26$.

- ☐ 45; 60; 180; 200
- ☐ 200; 180; 60; 54
- ☐ 6; 45; 180; 200
- ☐ 200; 60; 180; 54
- ☐ 0; 54; 180; 200

**17.** Select all of the ways you can use breaking apart and the Distributive Property to find the product of $35 \times 12$.

- ☐ $35 \times (10 + 2)$
- ☐ $(12 \times 30) + (12 \times 5)$
- ☐ $(12 \times 5) + (35 \times 5)$
- ☐ $(30 \times 5) + (10 \times 2)$
- ☐ $(30 \times 10) + (5 \times 10) + (30 \times 2) + (5 \times 2)$

Name_____

☆ ★ ☆
Solve & Share

There are 11 regular players and 5 substitute players on a soccer team. How many players are on 15 soccer teams? **Solve this problem using any strategy you choose.**

You can use structure and what you know about the Distributive Property and area models to find the product. *Show your work in the space below!*

**I can ...**
use place value and partial products to multiply.

**I can also** look for patterns to solve problems.

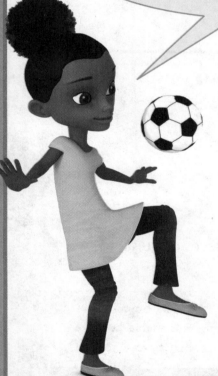

**Look Back!** How could you use an array and rounding or an array and compatible numbers to estimate the product for the problem above?

**A**

*Marcia put 7 oranges and 8 apples into each of 12 bags. How many pieces of fruit did Marcia put into all of the bags?*

Some problems have more than one step to solve.

$7 + 8 = f$
$15 = f$

Marcia put 15 pieces of fruit in each of the 12 bags.

$10 \times 10 = 100$    $10 \times 5 = 50$

15

12

$2 \times 10 = 20$    $2 \times 5 = 10$

**B**

Find $12 \times 15$.

Estimate: $12 \times 15$ is about $10 \times 15 = 150$.

First, multiply the ones.

$$\begin{array}{r} 15 \\ \times\ 12 \\ \hline 10 \quad 2\times 5 \text{ ones} \\ 20 \quad 2\times 1 \text{ ten} \end{array}$$

10 and 20 are partial products.

**C**

Then, multiply the tens.

$$\begin{array}{r} 15 \\ \times\ 12 \\ \hline 10 \\ 20 \\ 50 \quad 10\times 5 \text{ ones} \\ +\ 100 \quad 10\times 1 \text{ ten} \\ \hline 180 \end{array}$$

Marcia put 180 pieces of fruit into the bags.

50 and 100 are partial products.

The answer is reasonable because 180 is close to 150.

**Convince Me!** **Reasoning** Which partial products are incorrect? What is the correct final product?

$$\begin{array}{r} 26 \\ \times\ 12 \\ \hline 12 \\ 40 \\ 600 \\ +\ 2000 \\ \hline 2{,}652 \end{array}$$

Name _____

# ☆ Guided Practice

## Do You Understand?

**1.** In the example on the previous page, why do you find $2 \times 1$ ten, rather than $2 \times 1$?

**2.** In the example on the previous page, could you record the 4 partial products in a different order? Explain.

## Do You Know How?

For **3–4**, find all the partial products. Then add to find the final product. Draw area models as needed.

**3.**    23
    × 14

**4.**    41
    × 25

# ☆ Independent Practice ☆

For **5–12**, estimate. Find all the partial products. Then add to find the final product. Draw area models as needed.

Remember to check if your final product is reasonable.

**5.**    34
    × 51

**6.**    73
    × 81

**7.**    64
    × 32

**8.**    26
    × 53

**9.**    38
    × 17

**10.**    34
    × 30

**11.**    19
    × 43

**12.**    19
    × 52

# Problem Solving

13. The Castillo de San Marcos is a Spanish fortress that was built between 1672 and 1695.

    a. Rounded to the nearest ten thousand, how many pesos did it cost to build the fortress?

    b. How many years did it take to build the fortress?

It cost 138,375 pesos to build this fortress.

---

14. **Construct Arguments** A school has 2 large patios. One is rectangular and is 24 feet long by 18 feet wide. The other is square and each side is 21 feet long. Which patio has a greater area? Explain.

15. **Higher Order Thinking** Show two ways to break apart the factors, and then find the product of 14 × 22.

---

✔ **Assessment Practice**

16. Which set of numbers has the missing partial product and the final product?

    $$\begin{array}{r} 13 \\ \times\ 62 \\ \hline 6 \\ 20 \\ \square \\ +\ 600 \\ \hline \square \end{array}$$

    Ⓐ 210; 836

    Ⓑ 18; 806

    Ⓒ 180; 806

    Ⓓ 18; 644

17. Select all the equations in which 12 is the missing factor.

    ☐ $b \times 14 = 336$

    ☐ $b \times 36 = 432$

    ☐ $18 \times b = 216$

    ☐ $39 \times b = 468$

    ☐ $21 \times b = 231$

Name_____

### Solve & Share

Five students set a goal to raise $500 from their charity walk. Sponsors donated $25 for each mile walked. By how much did these students exceed or miss their goal? *Solve this problem using any strategy you choose.*

**DATA**

| Student | Miles Walked |
|---------|--------------|
| Susan | 5 |
| Maxine | 5 |
| Charlie | 3 |
| Fillip | 4 |
| Rachael | 4 |

**I can ...**
make sense of problems and keep working if I get stuck.

**I can also** use addition, subtraction, and multiplication to solve problems.

### Thinking Habits

*Be a good thinker!
These questions can help you.*

- What do I need to find?
- What do I know?
- What's my plan for solving the problem?
- What else can I try if I get stuck?
- How can I check that my solution makes sense?

**Look Back!** **Make Sense and Persevere** Is there more than one way to solve the problem? Explain.

**A**

*The park has a large garden with a walkway around it. The park's ground crew are going to paint the walkway. What is the area of the walkway?*

85 ft

32 ft   52 ft

65 ft

**What is a good plan for solving this problem?**

I need to find the area of the garden and walkway together. Then I need to subtract to find only the area of the walkway.

---

**B** **How can I make sense of and solve this problem?**

**I can**

- identify the quantities given.

- understand how the quantities are related.

- choose and implement an appropriate strategy.

- check to be sure my work and answer make sense.

**C** First find the area of the whole park.

$52 \times 85 = p$
$4{,}420 = p$

Next, find the area of the of the garden.

$32 \times 65 = g$
$2{,}080 = g$

Subtract to find the area of the walkway.
$4{,}420 - 2{,}080 = w$

The area of the walkway is 2,340 square feet.

$$
\begin{array}{r}
85 \\
\times \phantom{0}52 \\
\hline
10 \\
160 \\
250 \\
+ 4{,}000 \\
\hline
4{,}420 \\
\end{array}
$$

$$
\begin{array}{r}
65 \\
\times \phantom{0}32 \\
\hline
10 \\
120 \\
150 \\
+ 1{,}800 \\
\hline
2{,}080 \\
\end{array}
$$

$$
\begin{array}{r}
^{3\,12}\\
4{,}\cancel{4}20 \\
- 2{,}080 \\
\hline
2{,}340 \\
\end{array}
$$

---

**Convince Me!** **Make Sense and Persevere** Can you solve the problem a different way and still calculate the same answer? Explain.

Name_____

# ☆Guided Practice

## Make Sense and Persevere

On her vacation, Julia filled 3 memory cards like the one shown. She printed 2 copies of each picture. How many pictures did Julia print?

MEMORY

A memory card holds 28 pictures.

**1.** What do you know and what do you need to find?

When you make sense and persevere, you regularly check if your work is reasonable.

**2.** What steps might you take to solve the problem?

**3.** How many pictures did Julia print? Explain.

# ☆Independent Practice ☆

## Make Sense and Persevere

Jarrod delivers 63 newspapers each Monday through Saturday and 78 newspapers each Sunday. Last month consisted of 4 Sundays and 26 other days. How many newspapers did Jarrod deliver last month? Use Exercises 4–6 to solve this problem.

**4.** What strategies can you use to find how many newspapers Jarrod delivered last month?

**5.** How are the quantities related?

**6.** Explain how to solve the problem.

### Uniforms

The Stillwater Storm soccer team consists of 16 players. Each player needs a uniform set. The uniform set includes two jerseys, a pair of shorts, and a pair of socks. The price for each separate item is shown. Nine of the players need a medium size and the others need a small size. If the team buys more than 10 sets, the team price for each set is $56. How much money is saved if the team buys all the uniform sets together rather than separately?

| DATA | Uniform Item | Price |
|------|------|------|
| | Jersey | $23 |
| | Pair of Shorts | $17 |
| | Pair of Socks | $8 |

**7. Reasoning** What are the quantities in the problem and how are they related?

**8. Model with Math** Use the bar diagram to write an addition equation and find the total cost of the uniform sets when purchased separately. Then find the total cost if 10 sets or more are purchased.

*u*, cost of 1 set

| $___ | $___ | $___ | $_ |
|------|------|------|------|

When you make sense and persevere, you think about the amounts given.

**9. Be Precise** What is the difference in cost if the team bought all the uniform sets together or if they bought them separately?

Name _____

## Find a Match

Work with a partner. Point to a clue. Read the clue.

Look below the clues to find a match. Write the clue letter in the box next to the match.

Find a match for every clue.

**I can ...**
add and subtract multi-digit whole numbers.

**I can also** make math arguments.

**Clues**

**A** The difference is between 950 and 1,000.

**B** The difference is exactly 913.

**C** The sum is between 600 and 700.

**D** The sum is exactly 500.

**E** The difference is between 700 and 800.

**F** The sum is greater than 300 but less than 400.

**G** The sum is exactly 753.

**H** The difference is exactly 413.

|  |  |  |  |
|---|---|---|---|
| 571<br>+ 54 | 425<br>− 12 | 485<br>+ 15 | 283<br>+ 38 |
| 672<br>+ 81 | 818<br>− 93 | 994<br>− 24 | 986<br>− 73 |

# TOPIC 4 — Vocabulary Review

**Glossary**

**Word List**

- array
- compatible numbers
- estimate
- factors
- partial product
- product
- rounding
- variable

## Understand Vocabulary

**1.** Cross out the numbers that are **NOT** factors of 12.

1  3  5  6  8

**2.** Cross out the numbers that are **NOT** good estimates for the product of 17 × 23.

600  400  300  200  100

**3.** Cross out the numbers that are **NOT** partial products for 12 × 41.

2  10  18  80  400

Label each example with a term from the Word List.

**4.**  _____

**5.** *n* _____

**6.** 2,318 to the nearest thousand is 2,000 _____

**7.** 3 × 4 = <u>12</u> _____

## Use Vocabulary in Writing

**8.** Alicia needs to find 23 × 47. Use at least 3 terms from the Word List to explain how Alicia might find 23 × 47.

Name _____

## Set A  pages 129–132

Use place-value strategies to find 20 × 80.

Think about the pattern.

20 × 80 = 2 tens × 8 tens
       = 16 hundreds
       = 1,600

50 × 40 = (5 × 10) × (4 × 10)
       = (5 × 4) × (10 × 10)
       = 20 × 100
       = 2, 000

**Remember** when the product of a basic fact has a zero, there is one more zero in the answer.

Use a pattern to find each product.

**1.** 40 × 10          **2.** 60 × 20

**3.** 80 × 50          **4.** 30 × 90

**5.** 80 × 70          **6.** 60 × 60

**7.** 80 × 30          **8.** 20 × 50

## Set B  pages 133–136

Use an array or an area model to multiply 20 × 14.

← 20 groups of 10 = 200

← 20 groups of 4 = 80

200 + 80 = 280

So, 20 × 14 = 280.

**Remember** you can draw arrays or area models to represent multiplication problems.

Draw a model to find each product.

**1.** 10 × 23          **2.** 16 × 20

## Set C  pages 137–140

Use compatible numbers to estimate 28 × 19.

28 is close to 25.
19 is close to 20.

If 25 × 2 = 50, then
25 × 20 = 500.

So, 28 × 19 is about 500.

**Remember** that compatible numbers are numbers that are easy to compute with mentally.

Estimate each product.

**1.** 29 × 31          **2.** 42 × 49

**3.** 73 × 18          **4.** 24 × 38

**5.** 19 × 31          **6.** 63 × 87

Find 14 × 12. Draw a 14 × 12 array.

Separate each factor into tens and ones.
Color each section a different color.
Add each part to find the product.

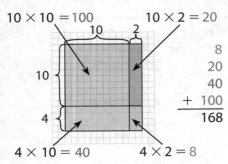

$10 \times 10 = 100$    $10 \times 2 = 20$

$$\begin{array}{r} 8 \\ 20 \\ 40 \\ + \ 100 \\ \hline 168 \end{array}$$

$4 \times 10 = 40$    $4 \times 2 = 8$

**Remember** when you break apart a multiplication problem, you can solve the simpler problems in any order and the answer will remain the same.

1. $14 \times 32$    2. $64 \times 12$

3. $56 \times 17$    4. $72 \times 15$

5. $26 \times 63$    6. $47 \times 27$

7. $19 \times 51$    8. $12 \times 56$

9. $76 \times 23$    10. $84 \times 37$

11. $14 \times 72$    12. $21 \times 51$

Use the Distributive Property to find 13 × 55.

$13 \times 55$
$= (10 + 3) \times (50 + 5)$
$= (10 + 3) \times 50 + (10 + 3) \times 5$
$= (10 \times 50) + (3 \times 50) + (10 \times 5) + (3 \times 5)$
$= 500 + 150 + 50 + 15$
$= 715$

**Remember** you can break numbers apart in more than one way when using the Distributive Property to solve multiplication problems.

1. $12 \times 19$    2. $38 \times 12$

3. $19 \times 25$    4. $45 \times 23$

5. $62 \times 11$    6. $46 \times 26$

Think about these questions to help you **make sense and persevere** in solving problems.

### Thinking Habits

• What do I need to find?

• What do I know?

• What's my plan for solving the problem?

• What else can I try if I get stuck?

• How can I check that my solution makes sense?

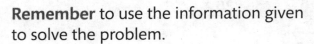

**Remember** to use the information given to solve the problem.

Rose visited 14 cities on her vacation. She bought 8 souvenirs in each city to send to her friends. Rose paid $2 in postage for each souvenir to be sent.

1. What hidden question do you need to answer to find how much it cost Rose to send all of the souvenirs?

2. How much did Rose spend on the souvenirs and postage?

Name_____

**1.** Don works 18 hours a week. Which expression shows a good way to use rounding to estimate how many hours Don will work in 52 weeks?

Ⓐ 10 × 50          Ⓒ 20 × 50

Ⓑ 10 × 60          Ⓓ 18 × 60

**2.** Find the product 21 × 40. Show your work.

**3.** The product of two factors is 2,000. One of the factors is 50. What is the other factor?

Ⓐ 20          Ⓒ 200

Ⓑ 40          Ⓓ 400

**4.** Select all the expressions that are equal to 260.

☐ 23 × 10

☐ 20 × 10 + 3 × 10

☐ 13 × 20

☐ 1 × 20 + 3 × 20

☐ 10 × 20 + 3 × 20

**5.** A florist makes centerpieces. He puts 18 roses in each centerpiece. Which is the best way to use compatible numbers to estimate the number of roses the florist needs for 24 centerpieces? What is the exact number of roses?

Ⓐ 10 × 25 = 250; 360

Ⓑ 20 × 25 = 500; 432

Ⓒ 25 × 30 = 750; 672

Ⓓ 30 × 30 = 900; 784

**6.** Margo hiked 12 miles 13 times last month. She hiked 14 miles 12 times this month.

**A.** Draw arrays or area models to find the number of miles Margo hiked during the past two months.

**B.** Write and solve equations to represent your arrays or area models.

**7.** Liz makes necklaces. Each has 16 beads. Use the numbers in the box to complete the table.

| 50 |
| 90 |
| 160 |
| 480 |
| 1,440 |

| Number of Necklaces | Number of Beads |
| --- | --- |
| 10 | |
| 30 | |
| | 800 |

**8.** Justine's plant shop has 7 shelves. Each shelf holds 18 plants. Suppose she adds 2 more shelves to the shop. Write and solve equations to find the number of plants all of the shelves can hold. Check if your answer is reasonable.

**9.** Jack's landscape service charges $78 to plant a tree. What is the total cost to plant 18 trees on Tuesday and 23 trees on Wednesday? Write and solve equations.

**10.** Which of the following uses properties of operations to help find $27 \times 14$?

Ⓐ  $20 + 7 + 10 + 4$

Ⓑ  $20 \times 7 \times 10 \times 4$

Ⓒ  $27 + 14$

Ⓓ  $(20 + 7) \times (10 + 4)$

**11.** Lorin drew an area model to find $19 \times 15$. Write the partial product for each rectangle in the area model.

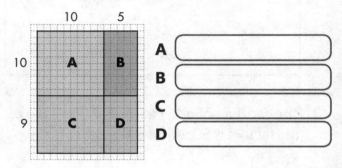

A [ ]
B [ ]
C [ ]
D [ ]

**12.** The biggest painting in an art show is 31 inches long and 28 inches wide. The smallest painting is 14 inches long and 11 inches wide. What is the difference between the areas of the two paintings? Use equations to show your work.

_____ square inches

Name_____

## Raising Money

The fourth-grade students at Skyline School sold candles to raise money. The money raised will be used to buy toys for children who live in a group home. The **Candle Fundraiser** table shows how many candles each class sold.

 Beehive candles sell for $20 each. The class raised $12 for each candle sold.

 Soybean candles sell for $22 each. The class raised $14 for each candle sold.

| Candle Fundraiser | | |
|---|---|---|
| Teacher | Number Sold | Amount Raised for Each |
| Mr. Li | 32 | $12 |
| Ms. Schmidt | 25 | $14 |
| Ms. Picard | 18 | $14 |
| Ms. Goldwasser | 47 | $12 |

1. About how much money did the fourth-grade students raise? Explain.

2. The school secretary needs to know exactly how much money was raised.

   **Part A**

   How much money did Ms. Schmidt's class raise? Use an area model and partial products to find the product.

## Part B

How much money did Ms. Picard's class raise? Use the Distributive Property to find the product.

## Part C

How much money did the fourth-grade students raise? Explain.

## Part D

Is the total amount of money raised from Part C reasonable based on the estimate you found in Exercise 1? Explain.

The fourth-grade students at Skyline School decide to buy the toys shown.

### Buying Toys

- They buy 68 toys in all.
- They buy at least 25 of each type.
- They cannot spend more money than was raised.

Teddy bear $17

**3.** How many of each toy can be bought following the directions from the **Buying Toys** list? Find the total cost for the numbers you choose.

Scooter $28

# Use Strategies and Properties to Divide by 1-Digit Numbers

**Essential Questions:** How can mental math be used to divide? How can quotients be estimated? How can the steps for dividing be explained?

Musical instruments make sounds when motion that causes vibrations creates sound waves.

This piano uses a series of keys and hammers to strike the strings, which play different notes depending on their length.

Instruments use energy to make sounds in all different ways! Here is a project about music and division.

## enVision STEM Project: Music and Division

**Do Research:** Use the Internet or other resources to find an example of a woodwind instrument, a brass instrument, a stringed instrument, and a percussion instrument.

**Journal: Write a Report** Include what you found. Also in your report:

- Explain how each instrument you researched uses energy to make sounds. Include information about how the sounds are produced.

- An octave spans 8 white keys on a piano. The last key of an octave begins the next octave. Explain why you can divide by 7 to find the number of octaves on a piano with 52 white keys.

Name _____

# Review What You Know

## A-Z Vocabulary

Choose the best term from the box.
Write it on the blank.

| • compatible numbers | • equation |
| • divisible | • round |
| • division | • variable |

1. A(n) _____ uses the equal sign (=) to show two expressions have the same value.

2. One way to estimate a product is to _____ each factor.

3. You use _____ when you find the number of equal groups.

4. Numbers that are easy to compute mentally are called _____.

## Division Facts

Find each quotient.

**5.** $27 \div 9$     **6.** $30 \div 5$     **7.** $32 \div 4$

**8.** $54 \div 9$     **9.** $28 \div 7$     **10.** $72 \div 9$

**11.** $56 \div 8$     **12.** $18 \div 3$     **13.** $15 \div 5$

## Rounding

Round each number to the nearest hundred.

**14.** 864     **15.** 651

**16.** 348     **17.** 985

**18.** 451     **19.** 749

> You will round or use compatible numbers to estimate quotients in this topic.

## Division as Sharing

20. **Make Sense and Persevere** Julio has 47 marbles. He keeps his two favorite marbles, then equally shares the remaining marbles between 5 friends. How many marbles does each friend receive? Explain.

Name_____

**PROJECT 5A**

**How many passengers did trains like those in the Gold Coast Railroad Museum carry?**

**Project:** Make a Model of a Train

**PROJECT 5B**

**How far do sailfish migrate?**

**Project:** Make a Migration Map

**PROJECT 5C**

**How much food do Portuguese Water Dogs need?**

**Project:** Create a Brochure on Portuguese Water Dogs

Before watching the video, think:

Healthy snacks are good for you. The best snacks include fruits and vegetables and whole grains. I wonder if I can feed this fish to my cat.

### I can ...
model with math to solve a problem that involves estimating, rounding, and computing with whole numbers.

Name _____

### Solve & Share

José has 270 hockey cards to arrange equally in 9 boxes. Each box can hold the same number of cards. How many cards should José place in each box? **Solve this problem using any strategy you choose.**

## Lesson 5-1
## Mental Math: Find Quotients

**I can ...**
make sense of quantities and use mental math and place-value strategies to divide.

**I can also** look for patterns to solve problems.

You can use structure and the relationship between multiplication and division. A multiplication fact can help you divide.

**Look Back!** **Reasoning** What multiplication equation could help you find the number of cards José should place in each box?

**A**

Mr. Díaz ordered a supply of 1,800 pastels. He wants to divide them equally among his class and 5 other art classes. How many pastels does each class receive?

If Mr. Diaz stores the pastels so each class will receive new pastels 5 times a year, how many pastels are handed out each of the 5 times?

1,800 pastels

Division is used to find equal groups. Dividend ÷ Divisor = Quotient

You can use basic division facts and place value to divide.

**B** Find 1,800 ÷ 6.

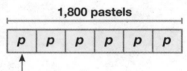

1,800 pastels

| p | p | p | p | p | p |

↑ pastels for each class

The basic division fact is 18 ÷ 6 = 3.

18 hundreds ÷ 6 = 3 hundreds or 300.
1,800 ÷ 6 = 300

Each class will receive 300 pastels.

**C** Find 300 ÷ 5.

300 pastels

| p | p | p | p | p |

↑ pastels given out 5 times

The basic division fact is 30 ÷ 5 = 6.

30 tens ÷ 5 = 6 tens or 60.
300 ÷ 5 = 60

Each class will receive 60 pastels 5 times a year.

**Convince Me!** **Use Structure** Write the missing dividends for each of the following equations. How did you determine each dividend?

_____ ÷ 7 = 70        _____ ÷ 8 = 50        _____ ÷ 4 = 800

Practice   Tools   Assessment

# ☆Guided Practice

## Do You Understand?

**1.** Explain how 32 ÷ 4 can help you solve 320 ÷ 4.

**2.** Mrs. Gall orders 240 folders and divides them equally among 3 classes. How many folders does each class receive? What basic fact did you use?

## Do You Know How?

For **3–4**, use basic facts and place value to find each quotient.

**3.** 28 ÷ 7 = _____
   280 ÷ 7 = _____
   2,800 ÷ 7 = _____

**4.** _____ = 64 ÷ 8
   _____ = 640 ÷ 8
   _____ = 6,400 ÷ 8

# Independent Practice ☆

**Leveled Practice** For **5–24**, use basic facts and place value to divide.

**5.** 36 ÷ 9 = _____
   360 ÷ 9 = _____
   3,600 ÷ 9 = _____

**6.** _____ = 10 ÷ 2
   _____ = 100 ÷ 2
   _____ = 1,000 ÷ 2

**7.** 45 ÷ 5 = _____
   450 ÷ 5 = _____
   4,500 ÷ 5 = _____

**8.** _____ = 24 ÷ 8
   _____ = 240 ÷ 8
   _____ = 2,400 ÷ 8

**9.** 2,000 ÷ 5

**10.** 360 ÷ 4

**11.** 540 ÷ 9

**12.** 160 ÷ 4

**13.** 900 ÷ 3

**14.** 3,200 ÷ 8

**15.** 360 ÷ 6

**16.** 1,800 ÷ 3

**17.** 7,200 ÷ 8

**18.** 500 ÷ 5

**19.** 350 ÷ 7

**20.** 6,300 ÷ 9

**21.** 1,600 ÷ 2

**22.** 210 ÷ 7

**23.** 4,800 ÷ 6

**24.** 600 ÷ 6

# Problem Solving

**25.** If you know 20 ÷ 5 = 4, how does that help you calculate 200 ÷ 5?

**26.** A bakery produced two batches of bread with 80 loaves in each batch. It sold 30 loaves each hour. How many loaves of bread were sold in 4 hours? How many loaves of bread were left to sell?

**27.** An engineer designed and built a solar race car. If there are 810 solar cells arranged in 9 rows, how many solar cells are in each row?

9 rows of solar cells

**28.** **Model with Math** On Saturday afternoon, 350 people attended a play. The seating was arranged in 7 equal rows. Draw a bar diagram and solve an equation to find *p*, how many people sat in each row.

**29.** **Higher Order Thinking** Molly and five friends picked a total of 300 oranges. If they each picked the same number of oranges, how many oranges did Molly pick? Explain.

## Assessment Practice

**30.** Find 240 ÷ 8.

Ⓐ 3
Ⓑ 10
Ⓒ 30
Ⓓ 80

**31.** What basic fact helps to solve 180 ÷ 6? What is 180 ÷ 6?

Ⓐ 18 ÷ 3; 60
Ⓑ 18 ÷ 3; 30
Ⓒ 18 ÷ 6; 60
Ⓓ 18 ÷ 6; 30

Name_____

## Solve & Share

Three friends at a video arcade win a total of 248 tickets. They decide to share the tickets equally. About how many tickets will each friend receive? *Solve this problem using any strategy you choose.*

You can use reasoning to estimate quotients using mental math. *Show your work in the space below!*

## Lesson 5-2
## Mental Math: Estimate Quotients

**I can ...**
use compatible numbers to estimate quotients when dividing with 3-digit dividends.

**I can also** reason about math.

**Look Back!** Is an exact answer or an estimate needed for the problem above? Explain.

**Essential Question**

# How Can You Estimate Quotients to Solve Problems?

**A**

*Max wants to make 9 rubber band balls using about the same number of rubber bands for each ball. He bought a jar of 700 rubber bands. Estimate to find about how many rubber bands Max can use for each ball.*

Max does not need to know the exact number of rubber bands to use for each ball. An estimate is all that is needed.

There is more than one way to estimate a quotient.

700 rubber bands

---

**B** **Use Compatible Numbers**

Estimate 700 ÷ 9.

What number close to 700 is easily divided by 9?

Try multiples of ten near 700.
710 is not easily divided by 9.
720 is 72 tens and can be divided by 9.
720 ÷ 9 = 80

Max can use about 80 rubber bands for each ball.

**C** **Use Multiplication**

Estimate 700 ÷ 9.

9 times what number is about 700?

9 × 8 = 72, so 9 × 80 = 720.
700 ÷ 9 is about 80.

Max can use about 80 rubber bands for each ball.

---

**Convince Me!** **Construct Arguments** What compatible numbers can you use to estimate 132 ÷ 6? Why is rounding not a good way to estimate 132 ÷ 6?

---

Name_____

#  Guided Practice

## Do You Understand?

**1.** Max wants to make 9 rubber band balls using 80 bands each from his package of 700. Will Max be able to make more or fewer balls than he wanted?

**2.** Max decides to use 700 rubber bands to make 8 balls. Is it reasonable to say he would use about 90 rubber bands to make each ball? Explain.

## Do You Know How?

For **3–10**, estimate each quotient. Use multiplication or compatible numbers. Show your work.

**3.** 48 ÷ 5

**4.** 235 ÷ 8

**5.** 547 ÷ 6

**6.** 192 ÷ 5

**7.** 662 ÷ 8

**8.** 362 ÷ 3

**9.** 41 ÷ 2

**10.** 211 ÷ 4

# Independent Practice

For **11–26**, estimate each quotient.

Think of basic multiplication facts to help find compatible numbers.

**11.** 430 ÷ 9

**12.** 620 ÷ 7

**13.** 138 ÷ 5

**14.** 232 ÷ 6

**15.** 342 ÷ 8

**16.** 652 ÷ 6

**17.** 59 ÷ 9

**18.** 813 ÷ 8

**19.** 637 ÷ 6

**20.** 481 ÷ 4

**21.** 747 ÷ 8

**22.** 232 ÷ 9

**23.** 552 ÷ 7

**24.** 52 ÷ 5

**25.** 392 ÷ 2

**26.** 625 ÷ 3

# Problem Solving

For **27–28**, use the table at the right.

**27.** Ada sold her mugs in 3 weeks. About how many mugs did Ada sell each week?

**Mugs Sold in Fundraiser**
Each Mug = 50 mugs

| Ada | |
| Ben | |

**28.** Ben sold his mugs in 6 weeks. About how many mugs did Ben sell each week?

**29.** **enVision®** STEM  The International Space Station takes 644 minutes to orbit Earth 7 times. About how long does each orbit take?

**30.** There are 60 minutes in 1 hour and 24 hours in 1 day. About how many times does the International Space Station orbit Earth each day?

7 orbits take
644 minutes

**31.** **Construct Arguments**  Complete by writing > or < in the ◯. Without dividing, explain how you know which quotient is greater.

930 ÷ 4 ◯ 762 ÷ 4

**32.** **Higher Order Thinking**  Explain how to find a better estimate for 260 ÷ 5 than the one shown below.

Round 260 to 300, and then estimate 300 ÷ 5.

300 ÷ 5 = 60, so 260 ÷ 5 is about 60.

---

**Assessment Practice**

**33.** Kaylee wanted to divide 133 pieces of candy equally into 7 boxes. She decides to put 19 pieces in each box. Use estimation to determine if this answer seems reasonable.

Name_____

### Solve & Share

Jimi has 3,000 tickets to sell at the school carnival. Jimi separated the tickets into groups of 8 tickets. About how many groups did Jimi make? *Solve this problem using any strategy you choose.*

You can use reasoning and compatible numbers to estimate. Dividing with compatible numbers makes estimating easier.

**I can ...**
estimate quotients for 4-digit dividends.

**I can also** reason about math.

**Look Back!** **Reasoning** What basic fact did you use to solve the problem above? How does this help you?

**Essential Question** **How Can You Estimate Quotients Using Patterns and Place Value?**

A

On "Clean Up Your Town Day," 1,320 people volunteered to clean up the Springville parks. The volunteers were divided equally into teams to work in each of the town's parks. About how many people were on each team?

Multiplication and division are related. Mentally multiplying by tens or hundreds can help to estimate the quotient of a multi-digit division problem.

Springville's parks

---

B **Use Multiplication Patterns**

Estimate 1,320 ÷ 6.

6 times what number is about 1,320?

You know $6 \times 2 = 12$, and
$\qquad 6 \times 20 = 120$, so
$\qquad 6 \times 200 = 1,200$.

1,200 is close to 1,320.

There are about 200 people on each team.

C **Use Division Facts and Place-Value Patterns**

Find compatible numbers to estimate 1,320 ÷ 6.

You know $12 \div 6 = 2$, and
$\qquad 120 \div 6 = 20$, so
$\qquad 1,200 \div 6 = 200$.

1,320 ÷ 6 is about 200.

There are about 200 people on each team.

---

**Convince Me!** **Construct Arguments** Complete the calculations at the right. Explain how you can use the calculations to estimate 1,296 ÷ 4.

$4 \times 100 =$ _____

$4 \times 200 =$ _____

$4 \times 300 =$ _____

$4 \times 400 =$ _____

---

**178** **Topic 5** | Lesson 5-3

Name _____

## Another Example!

You can use rounding to estimate quotients.

Estimate 357 ÷ 8 by rounding the dividend.

Round: 400 ÷ 8
400 ÷ 8 = 50
So, 357 ÷ 8 is about 50.

Estimate 5,582 ÷ 7 by rounding the dividend.

Round: 5,600 ÷ 7
5,600 ÷ 7 = 800
So, 5,582 ÷ 7 = is about 800.

## ☆ Guided Practice

### Do You Understand?

1. When estimating 1,320 ÷ 6, why is rounding not a good strategy?

2. When dividing a 4-digit number by a 1-digit number, how many digits can the quotient have?

### Do You Know How?

For **3–8**, estimate each quotient.

**3.** 3,340 ÷ 8        **4.** 2,943 ÷ 7

**5.** 552 ÷ 9          **6.** 776 ÷ 4

**7.** 2,013 ÷ 5        **8.** 281 ÷ 3

## ☆ Independent Practice ☆

For **9–20**, estimate each quotient.

**9.** 61 ÷ 2            **10.** 7,779 ÷ 7      **11.** 3,688 ÷ 6      **12.** 497 ÷ 8

**13.** 5,684 ÷ 9        **14.** 5,346 ÷ 6      **15.** 508 ÷ 7        **16.** 92 ÷ 3

**17.** 647 ÷ 3          **18.** 3,958 ÷ 8      **19.** 224 ÷ 3        **20.** 2,438 ÷ 5

# Problem Solving

**21.** Laura's dog eats 1 bag of dog food every 6 days. About how many bags will her dog eat in 1 year? About how many bags will Laura's dog eat in 10 years? Explain.

**22. Model with Math** During the school year, a bus driver made 7 trips to the museum. The distance from the school to the museum is 36 miles. Write and solve equations to find how many miles the bus driver drove for the 7 trips.

**23.** (A-Z) **Vocabulary** Use a vocabulary word to complete the statement.

Multiplication and division are _____ operations because they undo each other.

**24.** Ramón's sister wants to buy a car that costs $7,993. She earns $9 for every hour she works. About how many hours must Ramón's sister work to earn enough money to buy the car?

**25. Number Sense** Eight students can sit at one cafeteria table. About how many tables are needed for 231 students? Explain.

**26. Higher Order Thinking** At Camp Summer Fun, 4 campers share a tent. The camp is expecting 331 campers. About how many tents will they need? Will the actual number of tents needed be more or less than your estimate? Explain.

## Assessment Practice

**27.** Nadine has 1,424 pictures to put in 7 folders on her computer. She wants the same number in each folder. Which is the best estimate of the number of pictures she should put in each folder?

    Ⓐ  About 200

    Ⓑ  About 300

    Ⓒ  About 2,000

    Ⓓ  About 3,000

**28.** Sven needs to save $239 to buy a bike. Which is the best estimate of the amount he needs to save each month to have enough in 3 months?

    Ⓐ  About $60

    Ⓑ  About $70

    Ⓒ  About $80

    Ⓓ  About $90

Name_____

Activity

**Solve & Share**

There are 47 students taking a field trip. The students are being driven in cars to a play by adult volunteers. Each driver can take at most 4 students. How many cars are needed for the field trip? Will each car have four students? Use counters or draw pictures to solve this problem. Explain how you found your answer.

**I can ...**
apply what I know about dividing items into equal groups to solve problems.

**I can also** make math arguments.

You can draw a picture to model with math. *Show your work in the space below!*

**Look Back!** Suppose there were only 46 students. Would the number of cars needed for the field trip change? Explain.

# After Dividing, What Do You Do with the Remainder?

**A**

When you divide with whole numbers, any whole number that remains after the division is complete is called the **remainder**.

Ned has 27 soccer cards in an album. He put 6 cards on each page. He knows $27 \div 6 = 4$ with 3 left over, because $6 \times 4 = 24$ and $24 + 3 = 27$.

Use an R to represent the remainder: $27 \div 6 = 4\ R3$

How do you use the remainder to answer questions about division?

*The remainder must be less than the divisor.*

**B** *How many pages did Ned fill?*

To answer this question, find how many groups of 6 there are. The remainder can be ignored.

$27 \div 6 = 4\ R3$

Ned filled 4 pages.

**C** *How many pages did Ned work on?*

To answer this question, find how many groups of 6 are filled or started. Because there is a remainder, add 1 to the quotient.

$27 \div 6 = 4\ R3$

Ned worked on 5 pages.

**D** *How many cards did Ned put on the fifth page?*

The answer to this question is the remainder.

$27 \div 6 = 4\ R3$

Ned put 3 cards on the fifth page.

**Convince Me!** **Critique Reasoning** The calculation to the right is incorrect. What error was made? What is the correct answer?

$45 \div 6 = 6\ R9$

## Another Example!

There are 20 apples to arrange in gift baskets, with 6 apples in each basket. How many baskets can be filled? Explain the meaning of the remainder.

3 equal groups of 6 with 2 left over

$20 \div 3 = 6$ R2, because
$3 \times 6 = 18$ and $18 + 2 = 20$.

The remainder, 2, represents the number of apples not placed into gift baskets.

## Guided Practice

### Do You Understand?

1. When a divisor is 3, can the remainder be 5? Explain.

2. Dave is packing 23 sweaters into boxes. Each box will hold 3 sweaters. How many boxes will he need? Explain how the remainder affects your answer.

### Do You Know How?

For **3–6**, find the number of groups and the number left over. Draw an array if needed.

3. $47 \div 3 =$ _____ with _____ left over

4. $29 \div 2 =$ _____ with _____ left over

5. $62 \div 5 =$ _____ with _____ left over

6. $86 \div 6 =$ _____ with _____ left over

## Independent Practice

For **7–10**, find the number of groups and the number left over.

7. $18 \div 4 =$ _____ with _____ left over

8. $22 \div 6 =$ _____ with _____ left over

9. $31 \div 8 =$ _____ with _____ left over

10. $32 \div 9 =$ _____ with _____ left over

For **11–13**, interpret each remainder.

11. 59 football cards
3 cards on each page

How many pages can Alex complete?

12. 55 baseball cards
4 cards on each page

How many cards are on the last page?

13. 84 stickers
5 stickers on each page

How many pages will have some stickers on them?

# Problem Solving

For **14–15**, use the table at the right.

**Ticket Exchange**

| Prize | Number of Tickets |
|-------|-------------------|
| Toy Car | 8 |
| Ring | 9 |
| Marble | 7 |
| Sticker | 4 |

**14.** Samuel has 85 prize tickets. How many marbles can he get?

**15.** Inez chose 8 rings and 12 stickers. How many tickets did she use?

**16.** Keiko makes necklaces like the one in the picture at the right. She has 19 blue beads and 13 red beads. How many necklaces can Keiko make? How many of each color bead will be left over?

**17. Critique Reasoning** Amanda calculated $34 \div 8 = 3$ R10. Is Amanda's answer correct? If not, what is the correct answer? Explain.

**18. Higher Order Thinking** Write a problem that requires adding 1 to the quotient when interpreting the remainder.

✓ **Assessment Practice**

**19.** There are 39 children at a park. They want to make teams with 9 children on each team. Two of the children go home. How many complete teams can they make? Explain.

You can draw an array to help solve the problem.

Name _____

## Lesson 5-5
## Use Partial Quotients to Divide

**Solve & Share**

Sally's bird feeder holds 6 cups of bird feed. How many times can Sally's bird feeder be filled using a 72-cup bag of bird feed? Use counters or draw pictures to solve this problem. Explain how you found your answer.

**I can ...**
divide by thinking about multiplication, estimation, properties, and place value.

**I can also** reason about math.

You can think about how many times you can take away groups of six from your original number.

Bird Feed
72 cups

**Look Back!** **Reasoning** How can you use multiplication to check your answer?

# How Can You Use Partial Quotients to Solve Division Problems?

**A**

*There are 3 seats in each row of an airplane for passengers. If there are 63 people boarding the airplane, how many rows of seats are needed for the passengers?*

How many groups of 3 counters can be taken away from 63?

63 counters

This bar diagram shows the problem, where *r* equals the number of rows.

You can divide by finding partial quotients until only a remainder, if any, is left.

63 people

3 | r

people in each row

---

**B | One Way**

$$\begin{array}{c} 1 \\ 10 \\ 10 \end{array} \Big\} \; 21 \quad \text{10, 10 and 1 are partial quotients.}$$

3)63    Estimate: How many 3s are in 63? Try 10.
− 30    10 groups of 3 is 30. 63 − 30 = 33
  33    Estimate: How many 3s are in 33? Try 10.
− 30    10 groups of 3 is 30. 33 − 30 = 3
   3    How many 3s are in 3? 1
−  3    1 group of 3 is 3. 3 − 3 = 0
   0

There are 21 groups of 3 in 63.

21 rows of seats are needed.

---

**C | Another Way**

Sometimes you can use a different first estimate.

$$\begin{array}{c} 1 \\ 20 \end{array} \Big\} \; 21 \quad \text{20 and 1 are partial quotients.}$$

3)63    Estimate: How many 3s are in 63? Try 20.
− 60    20 groups of 3 is 60. 63 − 60 = 3
   3    Estimate: How many 3s are in 3? 1
−  3    1 group of 3 is 3. 3 − 3 = 0
   0

There are 21 groups of 3 in 63.

21 rows of seats are needed.

---

**Convince Me!** **Use Structure** How can you use the relationships between multiplication and division to check your answer?

---

## Another Example!

Break apart 69 using place value. Use the Distributive Property to show 69 ÷ 3.

$$69 \div 3 = (60 + 9) \div 3$$
$$= (60 \div 3) + (9 \div 3)$$
$$= 20 + 3$$
$$= 23$$

60 + 9 = 69

## ☆ Guided Practice

### Do You Understand?

1. Harry used the model below to find 84 ÷ 4. Use the Distributive Property to show why Harry's strategy works.

### Do You Know How?

For **2-3**, use partial quotients to divide. Use counters or draw pictures as needed.

2. How many groups of 4 are in 48?

   4)48

3. How many groups of 6 are in 78?

   6)78

## Independent Practice ☆

For **4-9**, use partial quotients to divide. You may use counters or draw pictures to help.

4. How many groups of 6 are in 90?

   90 ÷ 6

5. How many groups of 5 are in 85?

   85 ÷ 5

6. 2)78

7. 3)88

8. 2)84

9. 3)57

## Problem Solving

**10. Model with Math** A collection of 64 stickers is placed into 4 equal piles. How many stickers are placed in each pile? Use the bar diagram to write and solve an equation.

64 stickers

| s | s | s | s |

↑
stickers in each pile

**11.** A chef is baking cookies for 3 parties. For each party, the chef uses the same number of eggs. She has 2 dozen eggs. What is the greatest number of eggs the chef can use for each party?

**12.** Show how to use the Distributive Property to divide 54 by 2 by breaking 54 into 40 + 14.

**13. Higher Order Thinking** Amanda wants to put some of her books on 4 shelves with 6 books on each shelf and the rest on 6 shelves with 3 books on each shelf. Can Amanda arrange her books this way? Explain.

42 books

### ✓ Assessment Practice

**14.** Select all correct combinations of partial quotients that can be used to find 96 ÷ 3.

- ☐ 30, 2
- ☐ 30, 10, 2
- ☐ 10, 10, 10, 2
- ☐ 10, 10, 10, 6
- ☐ 20, 10, 2

**15.** Use the Distributive Property to find 84 ÷ 7. Which is the missing number?

$$84 \div 7 = (70 + \boxed{\phantom{x}}) \div 7$$
$$= (70 \div 7) + (\boxed{\phantom{x}} \div 7)$$
$$= 10 + 2$$
$$= 12$$

- Ⓐ 4
- Ⓑ 14
- Ⓒ 24
- Ⓓ 34

Name_____

☆ ☆
**Solve & Share**

The new reading room in the library is 9 feet long. It is divided into a reading area and a help desk area. It has a total area of 153 square feet. What is the total width of the new reading room? Use the model to help solve this problem. **Solve this problem using any strategy you choose.**

Activity

**I can ...**
divide by thinking about multiplication, estimation, and place value.

**I can also** reason about math.
Content Standard 4.NBT.B.6
Mathematical Practices MP.2, MP.7

|  | 10 feet | f feet |
|---|---|---|
| 9 feet | Reading area | Help desk area |

You can use what you know about place value and the relationship between multiplication and division to help solve the problem.

**Look Back!** **Reasoning** If the area of the reading room was 216 square feet and the length was still 9 feet, would the width be more or less than 20? Explain.

Essential Question

# How Can You Use Partial Quotients to Divide Greater Dividends?

**A**

A total of 277 people signed up to audition for a talent show. Five people at a time were brought in for a group interview. How many group interviews were needed to audition all 277 people?

TALENT SHOW TRYOUTS

Interview Room

 You can estimate and use partial quotients to divide.

There are 5 people in each group interview.

---

**B** Find 277 ÷ 5.

How many 5s are in 277?

Estimate:
40 × 5 = 200
50 × 5 = 250
60 × 5 = 300
60 is too many.
There are at least fifty 5s in 277.

$$\begin{array}{r} 50 \\ 5\overline{)277} \\ -250 \\ \hline 27 \end{array}$$

|    | 50  | n  |
|----|-----|----|
| 5  | 250 | 27 |

**C** How many 5s are in 27?

Estimate:
5 × 5 = 25
6 × 5 = 30
6 is too many.
There are at least five 5s in 27.

$$\begin{array}{r} 5 \\ 50 \end{array}\Big\} 55$$
$$\begin{array}{r} 5\overline{)277} \\ -250 \\ \hline 27 \\ -25 \\ \hline 2 \end{array}$$

|    | 50  | 5  |
|----|-----|----|
| 5  | 250 | 25 |

**D** There are no more 5s in 277.

277 ÷ 5 = 55 R2

There were 55 group interviews with 5 people in each group. Two people remain. A total of 56 group interviews were needed to audition all 277 people.

 Divide until the remainder is less than the divisor!

---

**Convince Me!** **Use Structure** How can you use multiplication and addition to check the answer above?

---

Practice  Tools  Assessment

## Another Example!

Find 1,968 ÷ 6.

| | 300 | 20 | 8 |
|---|---|---|---|
| 6 | 1,800 | 120 | 48 |

1,968 ÷ 6 = 328

$$
\begin{array}{r}
8 \\
20 \\
300 \\
\end{array} \Big\} 328
$$

$$6)\overline{1,968}$$
$$-1,800$$
$$\phantom{-}168$$
$$-120$$
$$\phantom{-}48$$
$$-48$$
$$\phantom{-}0$$

There are at least three hundred 6s in 1,968.

There are at least twenty 6s in 168.

There are eight 6s in 48.

You can use multiplication, estimation, and place value to help solve division problems!

## ☆ Guided Practice

### Do You Understand?

**1.** Hilary has 254 tokens to use for games at Pizza Mania. She would like to use an equal number of tokens for each of 3 visits she has planned. Will Hilary be able to use the same amount of tokens for each visit?

### Do You Know How?

For **2–3**, use partial quotients to divide.

**2.** How many 4s are in 6,787?
6,787 ÷ 4

**3.** How many 5s are in 6,209?
6,209 ÷ 5

## Independent Practice ☆

For **4–11**, use partial quotients to divide.

**4.** 9)153

**5.** 8)450

**6.** 3)2,826

**7.** 7)9,428

**8.** 7)4,318

**9.** 4)8,457

**10.** 8)5,699

**11.** 3)4,567

# Problem Solving

**12.** After a state fair, three 4th-grade classes volunteered to clean up the trash from the fairgrounds. In total, they collected 1,281 pounds of trash. If each class collected the same amount, how many pounds of trash did each class collect?

**13. enVision® STEM** An electric car can travel 4 miles on one kilowatt hour of electricity. How many kilowatt hours of electricity would it take for Shawn to drive his electric car to his grandmother's house and back? Shawn lives 156 miles from his grandmother.

For **14–15**, use the table at the right.

**14. Number Sense** Use estimation to find which material allows the students to make the least number of headbands.

**15. Higher Order Thinking** How many headbands can the students make? Explain.

For each headband, the students need 7 beads, 9 inches of ribbon, and 3 buttons.

| DATA | Material | Amount the School Has |
|---|---|---|
| | Beads | 6,437 |
| | Buttons | 3,636 |
| | Ribbon | 3,870 inches |

## Assessment Practice

**16.** Select all correct combinations of partial quotients and a remainder that can be used to find 4,567 ÷ 7.

- ☐ 600; 50; 2
- ☐ 500; 10; 50; R3
- ☐ 500; 100; 50; 2; R3
- ☐ 600; 50; R17
- ☐ 600; 50; 2; R3

**17.** Which is the quotient?
3,858 ÷ 8

- Ⓐ 4,082 R2
- Ⓑ 472 R2
- Ⓒ 482 R2
- Ⓓ 481 R8

Name_____

★ ☆ ★
**Solve & Share**

A class collected $238 to be distributed equally to two charities. How much money will each charity receive? Use objects or draw pictures to help solve this problem. Explain how you found your answer.

**I can ...**
sort objects into equal-sized groups to divide.

**I can also** choose and use a math tool to solve problems.

Using appropriate tools like place-value blocks, drawings, or money, can help you divide. What tool is easiest for you to use?

**Look Back!** When might you need to divide something into equal groups in everyday life?

## Essential Question: How Can Place Value Help You Divide?

**A**

The craft club made 375 key chains. They sold 137 of the key chains at the school fair. The rest need to be packed into 2 boxes with the same number of key chains in each box. How many key chains will go in each box?

375 key chains

First, subtract to find how many key chains need to be packed.

$$375 - 137 = 238$$

You can use place-value blocks or draw hundreds, tens, and ones to show 238. Then divide.

**B** Find $238 \div 2$.

Divide the hundreds into two equal groups.

1 hundred in each group

**C** Divide the tens into two equal groups.

1 ten in each group

**D** Unbundle 1 ten for 10 ones. Divide the 18 ones into two equal groups.

119 keychains go in each box.

**Convince Me!** **Use Appropriate Tools** Tell how you would evenly divide the money shown among 4 people using only $10 bills and $1 bills.

Name_____

## Another Example!

Find $55 \div 4$.

Divide the tens equally into 4 groups.
Regroup 1 ten as 10 ones and then divide
the ones equally into 4 groups.
There are 3 ones left over.

$55 \div 4 = 13$ R3

## ☆ Guided Practice

### Do You Understand?

1. Draw a picture to explain why
   $423 \div 3 = 141$.

2. The art teacher displayed 48 paintings
   on 3 walls. If each wall had the same
   number of paintings, how many
   paintings were on each wall?

### Do You Know How?

For **3–4**, tell how many are in each group
and how many are left over. Use place-
value blocks or draw pictures as needed.

3. 176 magazines divided equally into
   5 boxes

4. 56 marbles divided equally into
   3 bags

## Independent Practice ☆

For **5–8**, use place-value blocks or a drawing to divide. Record remainders.

5. $71 \div$ ____ = ____ R2

6. ____ $= 176 \div$ ____

7. $46 \div 3$

8. $65 \div 4$

# Problem Solving

9. **Model with Math**  A company with 65 employees is moving to a new location. All of the employees are divided into groups of 5 for the move. Write an equation and find *g*, the number of groups used for the move.

65 employees

5

*g*

groups of 5

---

10. Maya used a drawing to divide 86. She made groups of 17 with 1 left over. Draw a picture to determine how many groups Maya made.

11. **Number Sense**  A science museum has 2,400 gemstones displayed equally in 3 cases. How many gemstones are in each case? What basic fact did you use to determine the quotient?

---

12. Mr. Harold has 268 books on 4 shelves in the classroom library. He has the same number of books on each shelf. To find the number of books on each shelf, he divided 268 by 4. How many books are on each shelf?

13. **Higher Order Thinking**  Five fourth-grade classes from an elementary school took a trip to the United States Capitol. There were 25 students in each class. At the Capitol, a maximum of 40 students were allowed on a tour at one time. What is the least number of tours needed so all the students were able to take a tour?

---

## ✓ Assessment Practice

14. Which division equation is represented by the drawing below?

   Ⓐ  $72 \div 6 = 12$

   Ⓑ  $62 \div 3 = 24$

   Ⓒ  $64 \div 3 = 24$

   Ⓓ  $72 \div 3 = 24$

15. What is the missing divisor?

   $2,244 \div n = 374$

   Ⓐ  3

   Ⓑ  4

   Ⓒ  6

   Ⓓ  7

Activity

## Solve & Share

Sara volunteers at a clothing recycling center. She packs T-shirts into bins for display. She packs the same number of T-shirts into 3 bins. How many T-shirts does Sara pack in each bin? She packs shorts into 2 bins with the same number in each bin. How many pairs of shorts does Sara pack in each bin?

**I can ...**
use place value and sharing to divide.

**I can also** be precise in my work.

Be precise. You can use math symbols, numbers, or drawings to help. *Show your work in the space below!*

| DATA | Plain T-shirts | Striped T-shirts | Shorts |
|---|---|---|---|
| Number to Pack | 34 | 48 | 45 |

**Look Back!** Explain how you can estimate answers to the problems above.

Essential Question

# How Can You Record Division With a 1-Digit Divisor?

**A**

Helen has 55 postcards. As an art project, she plans to glue the same number of postcards onto 4 poster boards. How many postcards can Helen put on each poster board?

You can use place-value blocks to solve the problem.

---

**B** Divide the tens.

Estimate: 55 ÷ 4 is close to 60 ÷ 4 = 15.

Think: 5 tens divided into 4 equal groups.

$$\begin{array}{r} 1 \\ 4\overline{)55} \\ -40 \\ \hline 15 \end{array}$$

There is 1 ten in each group and 1 ten and 5 ones left over.

**C** Divide the ones.

Trade the extra ten for 10 ones. The 1 ten and 5 ones make 15 ones. Think: 15 ones divided into 4 equal groups.

$$\begin{array}{r} 13 \ \text{R3} \\ 4\overline{)55} \\ -40 \\ \hline 15 \\ -12 \\ \hline 3 \end{array}$$

There are 3 ones in each group and 3 ones left over.

Helen can put 13 postcards on each of the poster boards. This quotient is reasonable since it is close to the estimate of 15.

---

**Convince Me!** **Reasoning** What does the remainder mean in the problem above?

---

Name_____

## Another Example!

Find 135 ÷ 2.

Estimate:
135 ÷ 2 is about
140 ÷ 2 = 70.

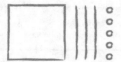

**What You Show**

- Regroup 1 hundred as 10 tens.
- Divide 12 of the 13 tens into 2 equal groups.
- Regroup 1 remaining or left over ten into 10 ones. Then, divide 14 of the 15 ones into 2 equal groups.

There is a remainder of 1.

**How You Record**

$$\begin{array}{r} 67 \text{ R1} \\ 2\overline{)135} \\ -120 \\ \hline 15 \\ -14 \\ \hline 1 \end{array}$$

13 tens divided into
2 equal groups
6 tens in each group
15 ones divided into
2 equal groups with
7 in each group.
Remainder of 1.

The quotient 67 R1 is reasonable since it is close to the estimate of 70.

## ☆ Guided Practice

### Do You Understand?

1. Explain how place-value blocks can help you with division.

### Do You Know How?

For **2–3**, estimate, and then find the quotient. Use place-value blocks or draw pictures as needed.

2. $5\overline{)82}$     3. $7\overline{)659}$

## ☆ Independent Practice ☆

For **4–11**, find each quotient. Use place-value blocks or draw pictures as needed.

4. $3\overline{)78}$     5. $3\overline{)86}$     6. $8\overline{)417}$     7. $4\overline{)93}$

8. $8\overline{)526}$     9. $7\overline{)88}$     10. $3\overline{)761}$     11. $6\overline{)96}$

# Problem Solving

**12.** Some of the tallest selenite crystals in a cave in Chihuahua, Mexico are 40 feet tall. Nathan is 4 feet tall. About how many times as tall as Nathan are the tallest crystals?

**13. Model with Math** The Galveston-Port Bolivar Ferry takes cars across Galveston Bay. One day, the ferry transported a total of 350 cars over a 5-hour period. The ferry took the same number of cars each hour. How many cars did it take each hour? Complete the bar diagram to help.

_____ cars

**14.** Zelda has a piece of fabric that is 74 inches long. She wants to divide it into 2 equal pieces. What is the length of each piece?

**15. Higher Order Thinking** Maggie is making trail mix. She makes 4 batches of the recipe shown. She divides it into 3 equal-sized bags. How many ounces are in each bag?

| Tasty Trail Mix | |
| --- | --- |
| Granola | 8 oz |
| Nuts | 5 oz |
| Raisins | 2 oz |
| Cranberries | 3 oz |

DATA

## ✓ Assessment Practice

**16.** Find the quotient.

7)784

- Ⓐ 112
- Ⓑ 114
- Ⓒ 121
- Ⓓ 122

**17.** Find the quotient.

60 ÷ 5

- Ⓐ 10
- Ⓑ 12
- Ⓒ 25
- Ⓓ 55

Name_____

Activity

Choose a strategy to solve each problem. Explain your solutions.

### Problem 1

There are 135 fourth-grade students. Each lunch table seats 6 students. How many tables are needed to seat all of the fourth graders?

### Problem 2

A high school football stadium has 5 sections. Each section seats the same number of people. A total of 1,950 people can be seated in the stadium. How many people can sit in each section?

**I can ...**
follow a series of steps that breaks the division into simpler calculations.

**I can also** reason about math.

You can use reasoning and estimating to see if the answers are reasonable. *Show your work in the space below!*

**Look Back!** **Look for Relationships** Are either of the problems above easily solved using mental math? Explain.

# How Do You Choose a Strategy to Divide?

**A**

**What strategy should I use to solve the problems below?**

HOT DOGS
8 Premium Hot Dogs

Think about which strategy you can use to solve the problem.

| Game Days Last Week | Number of Hot Dogs Sold |
|---|---|
| Saturday | 834 |
| Sunday | 216 |
| Monday | 75 |

DATA

**B** How many packages of hot dogs were used on Saturday?

Think: I can use partial quotients.

$$
\begin{array}{r}
4 \\
100
\end{array} \Big\} \; 104
$$

$$
8\overline{)834}
$$

$$
-\,800
$$

There are at least one hundred 8s in 834.

$$
34
$$

$$
-\,32
$$

There are four 8s in 34.

$$
2
$$

There were 105 packages of hot dogs used on Saturday.

**C** On Sunday, the 3 food stands each sold the same number of hot dogs. How many hot dogs were sold at each stand?

Think: I can break 216 apart and divide with mental math.

$$
\begin{aligned}
216 \div 3 &= (210 + 6) \div 3 \\
&= (210 \div 3) + (6 \div 3) \\
&= 70 + 2 \\
&= 72
\end{aligned}
$$

72 hot dogs were sold at each stand.

You can use the Distributive Property.

**Convince Me! Reasoning** How do you decide which is the best method to use?

## Another Example!

Only 75 cookies were sold on Monday, Tuesday, and Thursday. The same number of cookies were sold each day. How many cookies were sold each day?

$75 \div 3 = c$

$$\begin{array}{r} 25 \\ 3\overline{)75} \\ -60 \\ \hline 15 \\ -15 \\ \hline 0 \end{array}$$

7 tens divided into 3 equal groups. 2 tens in each group.
Regroup 1 ten as 10 ones. Now there are 15 ones.
15 ones divided into 3 equal groups. 5 in each group.

25 cookies were sold each day.

## ☆ Guided Practice

### Do You Understand?

1. Vickie's estimated quotient was 80. The actual quotient she calculated was 48. Is her actual quotient reasonable? Explain.

### Do You Know How?

For **2** and **3**, divide.

2. $9\overline{)2,871}$     3. $4\overline{)468}$

## Independent Practice ☆

For **4–11**, divide.

You can use different strategies to divide.

4. $8\overline{)3,288}$     5. $5\overline{)247}$     6. $6\overline{)1,380}$     7. $5\overline{)3,980}$

8. $6\overline{)367}$     9. $3\overline{)3,582}$     10. $4\overline{)756}$     11. $6\overline{)999}$

# Problem Solving

**12.** A family of four drove from San Francisco to New York. They drove the same number of miles each day for 6 days. How many miles did they drive each day? How can you interpret the remainder?

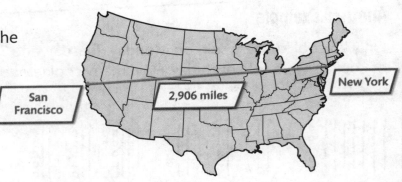

San Francisco

2,906 miles

New York

---

**13.** Without dividing, how can you tell if the quotient for 5,873 ÷ 8 is greater than 700? Explain whether the quotient is less than 800.

**14. Reasoning** A square dance set is made up of 4 couples (8 dancers). There are 150 people at a square dance. What is the greatest number of sets possible at the dance? Describe the steps you would take to solve this problem.

---

**15. Higher Order Thinking** Is rounding or using compatible numbers a more useful method when finding quotients in division problems? Explain.

**16.** Ron's Tires has 1,767 tires for heavy-duty trucks. Each heavy-duty truck needs 6 tires. How many heavy-duty trucks can get all new tires at Ron's?

---

## ✓ Assessment Practice

**17.** Select all correct equations.

☐ 565 ÷ 8 = 70 R5

☐ 3,613 ÷ 6 = 600 R13

☐ 3,288 ÷ 4 = 822

☐ 218 ÷ 3 = 72 R2

☐ 6,379 ÷ 7 = 911

**18.** Find 6,357 ÷ 8.

Ⓐ 814 R1

Ⓑ 794 R5

Ⓒ 794 R1

Ⓓ 784

Name _____

☆ ✩ ☆
**Solve & Share**

Allen set a goal to do at least 120 minutes of outdoor activities a day, Monday through Friday. He made a list of each activity and the amount of time he spends doing it every week. The same amount of time is spent every day doing the activities. Is Allen spending enough time each day on outdoor activities to meet his goal? What math can you use to solve this problem?

**I can ...**
use a drawing, diagram, or table to model a problem.

**I can also** use division to solve problems.

DATA

| Activity | Weekly Time in Minutes |
|---|---|
| Soccer | 200 |
| Bicycling | 150 |
| Walking | 300 |
| Running | 75 |

**Thinking Habits**

*Be a good thinker!*
*These questions can help you.*

• How can I use math I know to help solve this problem?

• Can I use pictures, objects, or an equation to represent this problem?

• How can I use numbers, words, and symbols to solve the problem?

**Look Back!** **Model with Math** What hidden question do you have to answer before you can determine if Allen met his goal? What math can you use to find the answer to this hidden question and the original question?

**Essential Question**

# How Can You Apply Math You Know to Solve Problems?

**A**

*A class is making decorations using same-size straws. They use the straws to make triangles, squares, pentagons, and hexagons. One package of straws is used for each group of polygons with the same number of sides. How many decorations can the class make?*

1,500 Paper Straws

## What math can you use to solve the problem?

I need to divide to find how many decorations can be made from one box of straws.

**B** How can I model with math?

**I can**

- use previously learned concepts and skills.

- find and answer any hidden questions.

- decide if my results make sense.

**C**

Here's my thinking.

Each polygon has a different number of sides.

I will divide 1,500 straws by the number of sides for each polygon:

$1,500 \div 3 = 500$ triangles     $1,500 \div 4 = 375$ squares

$1,500 \div 5 = 300$ pentagons   $1,500 \div 6 = 250$ hexagons

I will add all the decorations together:

$500 + 375 + 300 + 250 = 1,425$

The class can make 1,425 decorations.

**Convince Me!** **Reasoning** Another class made 200 octagon-shaped decorations. How many straws did they use?

# ☆ Guided Practice

Practice   Tools   Assessment

**Model with Math**

Miguel is going camping with 3 friends. He packed sandwiches for everyone to share equally. How many sandwiches did Miguel pack for each camper?

12 ham sandwiches

8 cheese sandwiches

20 peanut butter and jelly sandwiches

1. What hidden question do you need to solve first? Write and solve an equation to find the answer. Tell what your variable represents.

_____ sandwiches

2. Complete the bar diagram. Write and solve an equation to find the number of sandwiches, s, for each camper.

> You can use a bar diagram and write an equation to model with math.

# Independent Practice ☆

**Model with Math**

Jodi delivers 54 newspapers on Saturday and 78 newspapers on Sunday. She makes bundles of 6 newspapers. How many bundles does Jodi make on Saturday and Sunday combined?

3. Explain how you could use a picture to represent the problem and show the relationships. Define variables.

4. Write and solve equations to represent the problem. Explain how you can check that your solution is reasonable.

# Problem Solving

**☑ Assessment Practice**

**Dog Grooming**
Patricia and Antonio own a dog grooming business. To attract new customers, they offered free dog baths with the purchase of a grooming service. During the first 6 days of the promotion, they bathed 26 beagles, 12 boxers, 17 pugs, and 5 golden retrievers. Patricia and Antonio each bathed the same number of dogs each day.

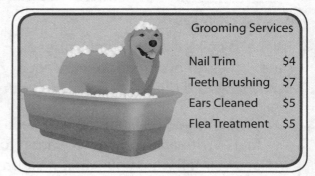

| Grooming Services | |
| --- | --- |
| Nail Trim | $4 |
| Teeth Brushing | $7 |
| Ears Cleaned | $5 |
| Flea Treatment | $5 |

5. **Reasoning** What are the quantities given in the problem?

6. **Make Sense and Persevere** What do you need to know to determine how many dogs Patricia bathed each day?

7. **Model with Math** Draw a bar diagram. Write and solve an equation to find *d*, how many dogs were bathed in all.

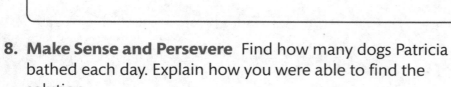

You model with math when you use a picture or equation to represent the problem.

8. **Make Sense and Persevere** Find how many dogs Patricia bathed each day. Explain how you were able to find the solution.

Shade a path from **START** to **FINISH**.
Follow the sums and differences that are
between 1,000 and 1,200. You can only
move up, down, right, or left.

TOPIC
5

**Fluency Practice
Activity**

**I can ...**
add and subtract whole
numbers with regrouping.

**I can also** be precise in my work.

| Start | | | | |
|---|---|---|---|---|
| 314 <br> + 707 | 7,020 <br> − 5,001 | 686 <br> + 304 | 1,064 <br> − 145 | 1,201 <br> + 289 |
| 4,300 <br> − 3,200 | 1,220 <br> + 99 | 4,054 <br> − 3,913 | 909 <br> + 402 | 1,509 <br> − 519 |
| 999 <br> + 200 | 3,099 <br> − 899 | 484 <br> + 750 | 1,580 <br> − 670 | 1,010 <br> + 1,101 |
| 3,455 <br> − 2,305 | 807 <br> + 499 | 3,704 <br> − 2,544 | 725 <br> + 460 | 1,388 <br> − 209 |
| 623 <br> + 500 | 2,010 <br> − 1,009 | 800 <br> + 350 | 1,577 <br> − 368 | 1,050 <br> + 99 |

Finish

**Word List**

- dividend
- division
- divisor
- equation
- partial quotients
- quotient
- remainder

## Understand Vocabulary

Choose the best term from the box. Write it on the blank.

**1.** The answer to a division problem is called the

_____.

**2.** The number to be divided in a division problem is called the

_____.

**3.** A way to divide that finds quotients in parts until only a remainder, if any, is left is using _____.

**4.** The number by which another number is divided is called the _____.

**5.** The operation that tells how many equal groups there are or how many are in each group is called _____.

For each of these terms, give an example and a non-example.

|  | Example | Non-example |
|---|---|---|
| **6.** equation | _____ | _____ |
| **7.** remainder | _____ | _____ |

## Use Vocabulary in Writing

**8.** Megan made 21 loom bracelets to share equally among her 7 friends. How many bracelets will each friend receive? Write and solve an equation. Use at least 3 terms from the Word List to describe your equation.

Name_____

**Set A** pages 169–172 _____

**Reteaching**

A school district shares 2,700 chairs equally among 3 school buildings. How many chairs will each school building have?

**2,700 chairs**

chairs for each school building

Find $2,700 \div 3 = c$.

The basic fact is $27 \div 3 = 9$.
27 hundreds ÷ 3 = 9 hundreds, or 900.
$2,700 \div 3 = 900$

Each school building will have 900 chairs.

**Remember** you can use basic division facts and place value to divide mentally.

**1.** $250 \div 5$        **2.** $810 \div 9$

**3.** $3,200 \div 4$        **4.** $4,200 \div 7$

**5.** $1,000 \div 2$        **6.** $240 \div 4$

**7.** $450 \div 5$        **8.** $720 \div 9$

**9.** $3,600 \div 4$        **10.** $4,900 \div 7$

**11.** $2,000 \div 2$        **12.** $280 \div 4$

**13.** $2,100 \div 7$        **14.** $560 \div 8$

**Set B** pages 173–180 _____

Use multiplication to estimate $420 \div 8$.

8 times what number is about 420?

$8 \times 5 = 40$,
so, $8 \times 50 = 400$.

So, $420 \div 8$ is about 50.

Use compatible numbers to estimate $1,519 \div 7$.

What number close to 1,519 is easily divided by 7?

Try division facts to help find compatible numbers for 1,519

1,519 is close to 1,400.

$14 \div 7 = 2$,
so $1,400 \div 7 = 200$.

So, $1,519 \div 7$ is about 200.

**Remember** basic facts can help you find a number that is easily divided by the divisor.

Estimate each quotient.

**1.** $718 \div 8$        **2.** $156 \div 4$

**3.** $482 \div 8$        **4.** $174 \div 3$

**5.** $843 \div 7$        **6.** $321 \div 2$

**7.** $428 \div 6$        **8.** $811 \div 9$

**9.** $5,616 \div 8$        **10.** $7,224 \div 8$

**11.** $6,324 \div 9$        **12.** $3,627 \div 9$

**13.** $331 \div 4$        **14.** $1,222 \div 6$

**15.** $2,511 \div 5$        **16.** $362 \div 6$

**17.** $4,940 \div 7$        **18.** $9,312 \div 3$

Tom is putting 14 apples into bags. Each bag holds 4 apples. How many bags can Tom fill? Will any apples be left over?

Use a model to represent 14 ÷ 4.

$$14 \div 4 = 3 \text{ R}2$$

Tom can fill 3 bags. There will be 2 apples left over.

**Remember** to make sure the remainder is less than the divisor.

1. 22 pickles
   3 pickles on each plate
   22 ÷ 3 = _____ with _____ left over

   How many plates have 3 pickles?

   _____

2. 19 stamps
   2 stamps on each envelope
   19 ÷ 2 = _____ with _____ left over

   How many stamps are not on an envelope?

   _____

Find 357 ÷ 7.

Use a model. Divide by finding partial quotients.

| | 50 | 1 |
|---|---|---|
| 7 | 350 | 7 |

$$\begin{array}{r} 1 \\ 50 \end{array} \Big\} 51$$

$$7)\overline{357}$$
$$\underline{-350}$$
$$7$$
$$\underline{-7}$$
$$0$$

Divide. Use the Distributive Property.
$$357 \div 7 = (350 + 7) \div 7$$
$$= (350 \div 7) + (7 \div 7)$$
$$= 50 + 1$$
$$= 51$$

**Remember** to add the partial quotients to find the actual quotient.

Use partial quotients to solve.

1. There are 81 chairs in 3 equal groups. How many chairs are in each group?

2. There are 174 games scheduled for 6 different leagues. Each league has the same number of games scheduled. How many games does each league have scheduled?

3. There were 1,278 people at the last basketball game. The stands were divided into 6 sections. The same number of people sat in each section. How many people sat in each section?

**Set E** pages 193–196

Margaret packed 68 books equally into 2 boxes. How many books did Margaret pack in each box?

Find 68 ÷ 2.

 68 books

Divide the tens into two equal groups. Then divide the ones into two equal groups.

68 ÷ 2 = 34, because 2 × 34 = 68.

Margaret packed 34 books in each box.

**Remember** to check if your answer is reasonable.

> Tell how many are in each group and how many are left over.

**1.** 138 books; 5 stacks

**2.** 55 shells; 3 jars

**3.** 217 pens; 7 cases

**4.** 154 shoes; 4 boxes

**5.** 195 seeds; 6 planters

**Set F** pages 197–200

Find 147 ÷ 6.
Estimate 120 ÷ 6 = 20.

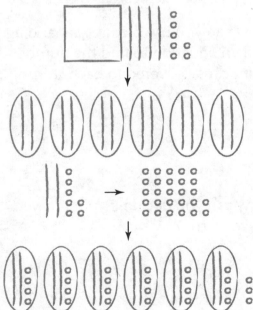

147 ÷ 6 = 24 R3 is close to 20, so the answer is reasonable.

**Remember** to estimate the quotient to check if your answer is reasonable.

**1.** 710 ÷ 9          **2.** 657 ÷ 5

**3.** 398 ÷ 8          **4.** 429 ÷ 2

**5.** 470 ÷ 6          **6.** 255 ÷ 4

Find 8,951 ÷ 8.
Estimate: 8,800 ÷ 8 = 1,100.
One strategy is partial quotients.

$$
\begin{array}{r}
8 \\
10 \\
100 \\
1{,}000
\end{array} \Bigr\} \;1{,}118 \text{ R}7
$$

$$
\begin{array}{r}
8\,)\overline{8{,}951} \\
-\,8{,}000 \\
\hline
951 \\
-\,800 \\
\hline
151 \\
-\,80 \\
\hline
71 \\
-\,64 \\
\hline
7
\end{array}
$$

**Remember** you can use your estimate to check if your answer is reasonable.

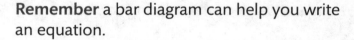

Choose a strategy to divide.

**1.** 4,649 ÷ 4     **2.** 2,843 ÷ 3

**3.** 8,478 ÷ 6     **4.** 6,399 ÷ 9

**5.** 379 ÷ 2     **6.** 3,812 ÷ 5

**7.** 4,793 ÷ 5     **8.** 5,957 ÷ 7

Think about these questions to help you **model with math**.

### Thinking Habits

- How can I use math I know to help solve this problem?

- Can I use pictures, objects, or an equation to represent the problem?

- How can I use numbers, words, and symbols to solve the problem?

**Remember** a bar diagram can help you write an equation.

A paint supplier delivered 1,345 cans of paint to 5 different hardware stores. Each store got the same number of paint cans. How many cans of paint were delivered to each store?

**1.** How can you use pictures, a bar diagram, and an equation to find the number of paint cans delivered to each store?

**2.** How can you decide if your answer makes sense?

Name_____

**1.** Select all the equations that are reasonable estimates for the quotient 184 ÷ 8.

☐ 160 ÷ 8 =20

☐ 200 ÷ 5 =40

☐ 180 ÷ 9 =20

☐ 150 ÷ 5 =30

☐ 180 ÷ 6 =30

**2.** Draw a bar diagram for the equation, and then solve.

2,400 ÷ 6 = m

**3.** Mrs. Bollis has two pieces of fabric to make costumes. One piece is 11 yards long and the other is 15 yards long. Each costume requires 3 yards of fabric. How many costumes can Mrs. Bollis make? How do the remainders affect the number of costumes she can make?

**4. A.** Write an equation to show how to divide 453 into 3 equal groups.

**B.** Complete the model to solve the equation in **A**.

**5.** What is the best estimate for 3,350 ÷ 8?

Ⓐ  600

Ⓑ  200

Ⓒ  400

Ⓓ  800

**6.** Draw an array and solve the equation.

$48 \div 9 = ?$

**7.** Use compatible numbers to estimate the quotient $530 \div 9$. Then find the exact answer.

**8.** Find $4,800 \div 6$ using a place-value strategy. What basic fact did you use?

**9.** Select all the equations in which the remainder is 5.

☐ $59 \div 9 = 6$ R?

☐ $352 \div 6 = 58$ R?

☐ $788 \div 9 = 87$ R?

☐ $1,486 \div 7 = 212$ R?

☐ $2,957 \div 8 = 369$ R?

**10.** Which of the following expressions does **NOT** have a remainder of 3?

Ⓐ $52 \div 7$

Ⓑ $123 \div 7$

Ⓒ $451 \div 7$

Ⓓ $794 \div 7$

**11.** Which of the following is **NOT** equivalent to $63 \div 3$?

Ⓐ $(60 + 3) \div 3$

Ⓑ $(33 + 30) \div 3$

Ⓒ $(60 \div 3) + 3$

Ⓓ $(60 \div 3) + (3 \div 3)$

**12.** Select all the quotients that are reasonable estimates for 472 ÷ 6.

☐ 450 ÷ 5

☐ 480 ÷ 6

☐ 500 ÷ 5

☐ 450 ÷ 3

☐ 1,200 ÷ 6 = 200

**13.** Use partial quotients to find the quotient. Choose numbers from the box to complete the calculations. Use each number once.

$$
\begin{array}{r}
6 \\
5\,0 \\
\square\,0\,0 \\
\hline
3)\overline{468} \\
-\,\square00 \\
\hline
16\square \\
-\,\square50 \\
\hline
\square8 \\
-\,1\square \\
\hline
0
\end{array}
\quad 1\square\square
$$

| | |
|---|---|
| 1 | 1 |
| 1 | 3 |
| 5 | 6 |
| 8 | 8 |

**14.** Find 1,600 ÷ 8. What basic fact did you use?

**15.** The fourth graders are going to the science museum.

| Group | Number of People |
|---|---|
| Mr. Vorel's Class | 30 |
| Ms. Cahill's Class | 32 |
| Mrs. Winter's Class | 29 |
| Miss Meyer's Class | 28 |
| Teachers and Chaperones | 18 |

Groups of 8 students can see a special exhibit on space travel. How many groups will be needed so everyone can see the exhibit?

**16. A.** Divide.

432 ÷ 8 = _____

**B.** How can you use the answer from Part A to find 4,320 ÷ 8?

**17.** The Pizza Stand gives patrons a free pizza when they collect 8 coupons. How many free pizzas can Mrs. Fowler get if she has 78 coupons? How does the remainder affect the number of free pizza's she gets? How many more coupons does she need for the next free pizza? Explain.

**18.** Estimate 257 ÷ 5. Explain how you can use multiplication to estimate the quotient.

**19.** Use an equation to show how to separate 128 into 4 equal groups. Explain how to check the answer using multiplication.

**20.** Write and solve an equation that shows one way to estimate 1,792 ÷ 6.

**21.** Draw a picture to explain why 657 ÷ 5 = 131 R2.

**22.** For each equation, mark a check to show the correct missing number.

| | 6 | 3 | 8 | 5 |
|---|---|---|---|---|
| 4,_00 ÷ 6 = 800 | ❏ | ❏ | ❏ | ❏ |
| 675 ÷ _ = 135 | ❏ | ❏ | ❏ | ❏ |
| 360 ÷ 6 = _0 | ❏ | ❏ | ❏ | ❏ |
| 98 ÷ 5 = 19R_ | ❏ | ❏ | ❏ | ❏ |

**23.** Holly uses 7 sheets of tissue paper to make one flower. If she bought a package with 500 sheets of tissue paper, about how many flowers will Holly be able to make? Use compatible numbers to estimate the number of flowers.

Name_____

**Saving What You Earn**

Trista's older brother Ryan got a job. Ryan would like to buy the items shown with his earnings. Ryan earns $8 for each hour he works.

1. Ryan is curious and wants to know the amount of time it will take him to earn enough money to buy the items shown.

**Part A**

How many hours does Ryan need to work to earn enough money to buy the computer? Explain how to use place value and mental math to solve.

$480

$341

$44

**Part B**

How many hours does Ryan need to work to buy the video game? Use a model to show how to find the quotient. Explain how to interpret the remainder.

**Part C**

How many hours will Ryan need to work to earn enough money to buy the smart phone? Use partial quotients to divide.

**2.** Ryan gets a raise. He now earns $9 an hour. Ryan decides to start saving for a car. He works 9 hours a week.

### Part A

How many hours does Ryan need to work to earn enough money to buy the car, as well as pay for the taxes, title, and plates as shown? Draw bar diagrams to help write and solve equations.

Used car: $2,793
Taxes, title, and plates: $235

### Part B

About how many weeks will Ryan need to work to buy the car and pay for the taxes, title, and plates? Explain.

### Part C

How many actual weeks does Ryan need to work to buy the car and pay for the taxes, title, and plates? Show your work. Explain why your solution is reasonable.

# Use Operations with Whole Numbers to Solve Problems

**Essential Questions:** How is comparing with multiplication different from comparing with addition? How can you use equations to solve multi-step problems?

It takes a lot of energy to power a neighborhood. Renewable energy can lower the pollution produced by powering these homes!

Some homes use solar power for energy. This type of renewable energy uses sunlight and is good for the environment!

Some of the energy is stored for nighttime or when it is cloudy. Here is a project on energy and multiplication.

**enVision** STEM Project: Energy and Multiplication

**Do Research** Use the Internet or other sources to find and describe 3 examples of renewable energy.

**Journal: Write a Report** Include what you found. Also in your report:

- Solar panels are made up of smaller modules or sections called cells. Find a picture of a solar panel. How many cells are in 6 solar panels? How many cells are in 9 solar panels? How many more cells are in the 9 solar panels than the 6 solar panels?

- Find examples of other items that use solar power.

# Review What You Know

**Vocabulary**

Choose the best term from the box.
Write it on the blank.

> • Associative Property of Multiplication
> • Commutative Property of Multiplication
> • compatible numbers
> • Distributive Property

**1.** The _____
_____ says that factors
can be multiplied in any order and
the product remains the same.

**2.** Breaking apart a multiplication problem into the sum or difference
of two simpler multiplication problems is an example of using the

_____.

**3.** According to the _____, factors can be
regrouped and the product remains the same.

## Dividing by 1-Digit Numbers

Estimate each quotient.

**4.** $16 \div 3$

**5.** $25 \div 4$

**6.** $155 \div 4$

**7.** $304 \div 3$

**8.** $1,283 \div 6$

**9.** $1,999 \div 4$

## Multiplying by 1-Digit Numbers

Find each product.

**10.** $53 \times 9$

**11.** $1,127 \times 7$

**12.** $2,769 \times 5$

**13.** $3 \times 215$

**14.** $914 \times 5$

**15.** $1,238 \times 5$

## Problem Solving

**16. Construct Arguments** Explain why the
array represents $3 \times 21$.

**17.** James multiplies 38 by 55. He finds three of the four partial products: 40, 150, and
400. Which partial product is James missing? What is the solution?

Name _____

Pick a Project

PROJECT
6A

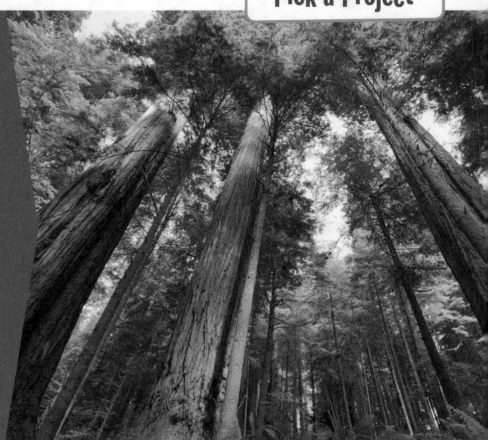

### How tall is tall?

**Project:** Model the Height of a Redwood Tree

PROJECT
6B

### What are some interesting number facts about a manatee?

**Project:** Make a Presentation with Manatee Number Facts

**PROJECT 6C**

### How does temperature affect an alligator egg?

**Project:** Create a Bar Diagram

**PROJECT 6D**

### How many eggs does the loggerhead turtle lay?

**Project:** Model a Turtle's Egg

Name _____

Activity

**Solve & Share**

Sarah is making a square pillow with edges that each measure 18 inches long. She needs a strip of fabric 4 times as long as one edge of the pillow to make a border around the pillow. How long does the strip of fabric need to be? *Solve this problem any way you choose.*

**I can ...**
use multiplication or addition to compare one quantity to another.

**I can also** model with math to solve problems.

Use reasoning to make sense of the quantities in the problem. You can use a bar diagram to understand the relationship between the quantities.

**Look Back!** **Model with Math** How could a bar diagram help you write and solve an equation for the problem?

# How Is Comparing with Multiplication Different from Comparing with Addition?

**A**

Max said the Rangers scored 3 times as many runs as the Stars. Jody said the Rangers scored 8 more runs than the Stars. Could both Max and Jody be correct?

STARS    RANGERS

BALL ··· STRIKE ·· OUT ··

You can use multiplication or addition to compare the number of runs made by each team.

Let $m$ = the runs scored by the Rangers according to Max. Let $j$ = the runs scored by the Rangers according to Jody.

**B** **Compare with Multiplication**

Find 3 times as many as 4 runs.

$m$

Rangers' total runs → | 4 | 4 | 4 |  3 times as many

Stars' runs → | 4 |

$m = 3 \times 4$
$m = 12$ runs

According to Max, the Rangers scored 12 runs.

**C** **Compare with Addition**

Find 8 more than 4 runs.

Rangers' total runs → | $j$ |

| 4 | 8 |

Stars' runs ↑    8 more runs

$j = 4 + 8$
$j = 12$ runs

According to Jody, the Rangers scored 12 runs.

Max and Jody are both correct.

**Convince Me!** **Construct Arguments** Describe when you would use multiplication and when you would use addition to make a comparison.

Name_____

# ☆ Guided Practice

## Do You Understand?

1. Use the information from the previous page. If the Rangers scored 5 times as many runs as the Stars, how many runs would the Rangers have scored?

   a. Compare using multiplication. Write and solve an equation.

   b. How could you use addition to compare the runs for the two teams?

## Do You Know How?

For **2–3**, complete the comparison sentence. Find the value of the variable that makes the sentence true.

2. Sam's baseball team has 4 times as many helmets as Ed's team. Ed's team has 21 helmets. Let $h$ = the number of helmets Sam's team has.

   $h$ is _____ times as many as _____.
   $h$ = _____

3. There are 128 more trees in the park than at Ty's house. There are 3 trees at Ty's house. Let $t$ = the number of trees in the park.

   _____ more than _____ is $t$. $t$ = _____

# Independent Practice ☆

For **4–9**, write a comparison sentence. For **4–7**, find the value of the variable that makes the sentence true.

Use *times as many as* or *more than* to compare the amounts.

4. Katy has 6 times as many nickels as Shaun. Shaun has 18 nickels. Let $n$ = the number of nickels Katy has.

   $n$ is _____
   $n$ = _____

5. Kyle has watched 238 movies. Jason has watched 49 more movies than Kyle. Let $m$ = the number of movies Jason has watched.

   $m$ is _____
   $m$ = _____

6. Amber tied 89 knots to make a macrame wall hanging. Hunter tied 3 times as many knots as Amber. Let $k$ = the number of knots Hunter tied.

   $k$ is _____
   $k$ = _____

7. Tia sells 292 newspapers. Tess sells 117 more newspapers than Tia. Let $n$ = the number of newspapers Tess sells.

   $n$ is _____
   $n$ = _____

8. Trent has 48 markers. Sharon has 8 markers.

   _____
   _____

9. Lucy has 317 bottles. Craig has 82 bottles.

   _____
   _____

# Problem Solving

**10. Model with Math** Roger swam 19 laps in the pool. Anna Maria swam 4 times as many laps as Roger. How many laps did Anna Maria swim? Draw a bar diagram and write an equation to solve the problem.

**11. Critique Reasoning** Nina says the equation $600 = 12 \times 50$ means 600 is 12 times as many as 50. Julio says the equation means 600 is 50 times as many as 12. Who is correct? Explain.

**12. Vocabulary** The amount that is left after dividing a number into equal parts is called the _____.

$13 \div 4 =$ _____

**13. Higher Order Thinking** A shirt is on sale for $d$ dollars. The regular price is 4 times as much. Todd has enough money to buy 2 shirts at the regular price. How many shirts can Todd buy at the sale price? Explain.

## Assessment Practice

**14.** Select all the sentences that involve a comparison using multiplication.

- ☐ $k$ is 26 times as many as 7.
- ☐ $u$ is 18 more than 314.
- ☐ Tom ran 4 miles. Cindy ran 2 more miles than Tom. How many miles did Cindy run?
- ☐ Yuhan has 2 dogs and Jon has 3 times as many dogs. How many dogs does Jon have?
- ☐ Kris has 4 times as many pairs of shoes as her brother. Her brother has 8 pairs of shoes.

**15.** Select all the statements that can be represented by the equation $5 \times 9 = w$.

- ☐ $w$ is 9 more than 5.
- ☐ $w$ is 5 times as much as 9.
- ☐ Henry sang 9 songs during practice. He sang 5 times as many as Joe, who sang $w$ songs.
- ☐ Greg carried 9 buckets of water to his sister's baby pool. His mother carried $w$ buckets, which was 5 times as many.
- ☐ Tom has 9 pens. Joan has $w$ pens, which is 5 fewer.

Activity

☆ ☆
**Solve & Share**

The students in Ms. Chang's fourth-grade class plant a tree every year. One tree they planted is now 288 inches tall. This height is 6 times as great as when the tree was first planted. How tall was the tree when it was first planted? *Solve this problem any way you choose.* Show your work.

**Lesson 6-2**
**Continue to Solve Comparison Problems**

**I can ...**
use multiplication or division to compare one quantity to another.

**I can also** model with math to solve problems.

288 inches

? inches

You can model with math and use equations to compare the heights of the two trees.

**Look Back!** Compare the heights of the 2 trees using addition.

**Essential Question** **How Can You Solve a Problem Involving Multiplication as Comparison?**

**A**

Carla and Calvin are twins that attend different colleges. Carla's college is four times as far from home as Calvin's college. How far does Calvin travel to college?

Carla travels 192 miles to college.

Let $m$ = the miles Calvin travels to college.

192 miles

| Carla | $m$ | $m$ | $m$ | $m$ |
|---|---|---|---|---|

4 times as far

| Calvin | $m$ |
|---|---|

Multiplication and division have an inverse relationship.

**B** The number of miles Carla travels, or 192 miles, is 4 times as far as Calvin travels.

Write a multiplication equation to find the number of miles Calvin travels to college.

$$192 = 4 \times m$$

What number times 4 equals 192?

**C** If $192 = 4 \times m$, then $m = 192 \div 4$.

$$\begin{array}{r} 8 \\ 40 \\ \hline 4)\overline{192} \\ -\,160 \\ \hline 32 \\ -\,32 \\ \hline 0 \end{array}\Big\} 48$$

| 4 | 40 | 8 |
|---|---|---|
| | 160 | 32 |

192

$m = 48$ miles

Calvin travels 48 miles to college.

**Convince Me!** **Use Structure** When do you use division to make a comparison?

# ☆Guided Practice

## Do You Understand?

**1.** Carla travels 3 times as far to college as her friend Mandy travels to college. Write and solve a related multiplication and division equation to find how far Mandy travels to college.

## Do You Know How?

**2.** Complete the comparison sentence. Find the value of the variable that makes the sentence true.

If $3 \times m = 48$, then $m = 48 \div 3$.

_____ times as many as

_____ is _____.

$m =$ _____

# Independent Practice ☆

> For **3–8**, write a comparison sentence and an equation. Find the value of the variable that makes the sentence true.

**3.** Connor has 77 magazines. That is 7 times as many magazines Kristen has. How many magazines, $n$, does Kristen have?

**4.** Eric completed 75 math problems. That is 5 times as many math problems as Katie completed. How many math problems, $m$, did Katie complete?

**5.** Clare counted 117 different colors at the paint store. That is 9 times as many as the number James counted. How many different colors, $c$, did James count?

**6.** Alisa has 153 dominoes. That is 3 times as many dominoes as Stan has. How many dominoes, $d$, does Stan have?

**7.** Justin practiced piano for $h$ hours. His sister practiced for 12 hours, which was 3 times as many hours as Justin practiced. Write and solve an equation to find how many hours Justin practiced piano.

**8.** Mary practiced violin for 2 hours and her brother practiced trombone $t$ times as long or 8 hours. Write and solve an equation to find how many times as long Mary's brother practiced trombone.

# Problem Solving

**9. Model with Math** Dave is making soup that includes 12 cups of water and 3 cups of broth. How many times as much water as broth will be in the soup? Draw a bar diagram and write and solve an equation.

**10.** Trevor wants to buy three light fixtures that cost $168 each. He has $500. Does he have enough money to buy the three light fixtures? Use a comparison sentence to explain your reasoning.

**11.** Miranda has 4 times as many leaves in her collection as Joy. Joy has 13 more leaves than Armani. Armani has 10 leaves in his collection. How many leaves does Miranda have in her collection? Explain.

**12. Higher Order Thinking** Jordan needs $9,240 for her first year of college tuition. Each of her two grandfathers said they would match what she saves. She has 8 years before she goes to college. How much does Jordan need to save on her own each year to have enough for her first year with the help from her two grandfathers?

Some problems require more than one operation.

☑ **Assessment Practice**

**13.** Tina walked 20 miles for a fundraiser. Lia walked $m$ miles. Tina walked 4 times as far as Lia. Which equation can be used to find $m$, the number of miles Lia walked?

Ⓐ $m = 4 \times 20$

Ⓑ $20 = 4 \times m$

Ⓒ $20 = m \div 4$

Ⓓ $m = 20 + 4$

**14.** Jason and Raul kept a reading log for the year. Jason read 7 books and Raul read 105. How many times as many books as Jason did Raul read?

Ⓐ 13 times

Ⓑ 14 times

Ⓒ 15 times

Ⓓ 16 times

Name_____

### Solve & Share

Last year, 18 people went on a family camping trip. This year, three times as many people went. How many more people went this year than last year? Complete the bar diagram and show how you solve.

You can make sense and persevere by finding and answering the hidden question.

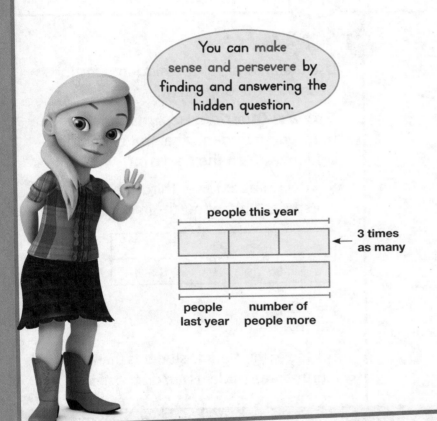

people this year

← 3 times as many

people last year     number of people more

**Look Back!** How can you use estimation to decide if your answer is reasonable?

**Essential Question** **How Can You Use Diagrams and Equations to Solve Multi-Step Problems?**

**A**

A school uses 8 buses to transport the fourth-grade students and 6 vans to transport the third-grade students on a field trip. How many fewer third-grade students than fourth-grade students are on the field trip?

Each bus holds 24 students.

Each van holds 15 students.

You can use variables or letters to represent unknown numbers in equations.

**B** **Step 1**

Find and answer the hidden questions.

**Hidden Question:** How many fourth-grade students are on the field trip?

**F = Number of fourth graders**

| 24 | 24 | 24 | 24 | 24 | 24 | 24 | 24 |

$F = 8 \times 24$
$\phantom{F} = 192$ fourth-grade students

**Hidden Question:** How many third-grade students are on the field trip?

**T = Number of third graders**

| 15 | 15 | 15 | 15 | 15 | 15 |

$T = 6 \times 15$
$\phantom{T} = 90$ third-grade students

**C** **Step 2**

Use the answers to the hidden questions to answer the original question.

**Original Question:** How many fewer third-grade students than fourth-grade students are on the field trip?

$S =$ the number fewer third-grade students than fourth-grade students

| 192 | |
|---|---|
| 90 | S |

$S = 192 - 90$
$\phantom{S} = 102$

102 fewer third-grade students than fourth-grade students are on the field trip.

**Convince Me!** **Construct Arguments** Amanda says she can solve the problem using the equation below. Do you agree? Explain.

$S = (8 \times 24) - (6 \times 15)$

## Another Example!

The Lopez family gets 2 pizzas and 4 hot dogs at Eat-It-Up. What is the total cost?

**EAT-IT-UP**

| Hamburger | $8 | Pizza | $18 | Turkey Wrap | $9 |
| Hot Dog | $6 | Salad | $16 | Drinks | $2 |

### Step 1

Write expressions to represent the hidden questions.

**What is the cost of 2 pizzas?**

| 18 | 18 |

$2 \times 18$

**What is the cost of 4 hot dogs?**

| 6 | 6 | 6 | 6 |

$4 \times 6$

### Step 2

Combine the expressions into an equation to find $T$, the total cost.

$T$ = Total cost

| 18 | 18 | 6 | 6 | 6 | 6 |

Cost of Pizzas    Cost of Hot Dogs

$T = (2 \times 18) + (4 \times 6)$

### Step 3

Solve.

$T = (2 \times 18) + (4 \times 6)$
$T = 36 + 24$
$T = 60$

The total cost is $60.

$2 \times 18$ and $4 \times 6$ are expressions.
$T = (2 \times 18) + (4 \times 6)$ is an equation.

## ☆ Guided Practice

### Do You Understand?

1. Doug says he can use the equation $T = 18 + 18 + 6 + 6 + 6 + 6$ to solve the problem above. Is Doug correct? Explain.

2. Write one or more equations you could use to find the total cost $C$, of 2 turkey wraps, 2 hamburgers, and 4 drinks.

### Do You Know How?

3. In the problem on the previous page, suppose the school fills 11 buses and lets the remaining students ride in vans. How many students ride in vans? Use one or more bar diagram and equation to show how you solve.

## ☆ Independent Practice ☆

Draw a bar diagram, and write an equation to solve the problem. Use a variable to represent an unknown quantity and tell what the variable represents.

4. Four boys and five girls went to the movies together. Between them they had $120 to spend. Tickets cost $8 each. How much money did they have to buy refreshments?

# Problem Solving

**5. Model with Math** A power plant has 4 tons of coal. A ton of coal produces 2,460 kilowatt hours of electricity. The plant reserves enough electricity to power 9 light bulbs for a year. How many additional kilowatt hours of electricity are produced? Draw bar diagrams and write one or more equations to show how you solve. Tell what your variables represent.

It takes 876 kilowatt hours of electricity to power a 100-watt light bulb for a year.

**6. Higher Order Thinking** You have $350 to buy 26 tickets for a baseball game. You need to buy some of each kind of seat. You want to spend most of the money. How many of each type of ticket can you buy? Find two different solutions to the problem. Use an equation to show each solution.

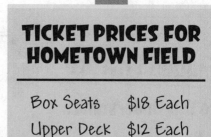

**TICKET PRICES FOR HOMETOWN FIELD**

Box Seats    $18 Each

Upper Deck    $12 Each

## ✅ Assessment Practice

**7.** The gym teacher has $250 to spend on volleyball equipment. She buys 4 volleyball nets for $28 each. Volleyballs cost $7 each. How many volleyballs can she buy? Explain how you solve. Use one or more equations and bar diagrams in your explanation. Tell what your variables represent.

**Solve & Share**

Three eight-year-old children, one adult, and one senior had $125 saved to go to the Happy Days amusement park. After buying tickets, how much money did they have left to buy refreshments? Complete the bar diagram, and use it to write one or more equations to solve the problem. Tell what your variables represent.

**I can ...**
Solve multi-step problems by drawing bar diagrams and writing expressions and equations.

**I can also** model with math to solve problems.

You can model with math by using equations and bar diagrams to find how much money the group had left.

## HAPPY DAYS
### TICKETS

Children under 5 **Free**
Children 6-12 **$12**
Teens **$20**
Adults 20 to 65 **$25**
Seniors **$18**

| | | | |
|---|---|---|---|
| Children | Adult | Senior | Refreshments |

**Look Back!** What expressions and equations did you use to solve this problem? What hidden questions did you need to answer?

**Essential Question**

# How Can You Model and Solve Multi-Step Problems?

**A**

Chef Angela needs 8 cartons of eggs to make the cakes that are ordered. She has 2 cartons of eggs and 4 single eggs in the refrigerator. How many more eggs does she need to make all of the cakes?

A carton has 12 eggs.

Multi-step problems can often be solved in more than one way.

The chef estimates she needs about 6 cartons or about $6 \times 12 = 72$ more eggs.

**B** ## One Way

How many eggs does the chef have?

$(2 \times 12) + 4 = 24 + 4$
$\qquad\qquad\quad = 28$ eggs

How many more eggs does the chef need?

$N$ = number of additional eggs needed

$N = (8 \times 12) - 28$
$\quad = 96 - 28$
$\quad = 68$

The expression $8 \times 12$ is how many eggs the chef needs in all.

The chef needs 68 more eggs.

Since 68 is close to 72, the answer is reasonable.

**C** ## Another Way

How many full cartons should the chef buy?

$8 - 2 = 6$ full cartons

How many more eggs does the chef need?

$N$ = number of additional eggs needed

$N = (6 \times 12) - 4$
$\quad = 72 - 4$
$\quad = 68$

The expression $6 \times 12$ is the number of eggs in 6 cartons.

The chef needs 68 more eggs.

Since 68 is a close to 72, the answer is reasonable.

**Convince Me!** **Model with Math** Draw bar diagrams to represent a solution to the problem above.

Practice  Tools  Assessment

# ☆ Guided Practice

## Do You Understand?

1. Explain the meaning of the expression $(2 \times 12) + 4$ in the problem on the previous page.

2. In the problem on the previous page, how many eggs will the chef have left over? Explain.

## Do You Know How?

3. Carrie's stamp book has 20 pages and each page can hold 15 stamps. She has 45 international stamps. She has 4 times as many U.S. stamps. Can all her stamps fit in her book? Use the bar diagram below to help solve this problem. Draw other bar diagrams as needed. Show the equations used to solve this problem.

?

| 45 | 45 | 45 | 45 | ← 4 times as many

| 45 |

# Independent Practice ☆

For **4–5**, draw bar diagrams, and write equations to solve each problem. Use variables to represent unknown quantities and tell what each variable represents.

4. Five toymakers each carved 28 blocks and 17 airplanes. Three other toymakers each carved the same number of airplanes and twice as many blocks. How many toys did the eight carve in all?

5. Kendra is using 27 blue patches and some white patches to make a quilt. The quilt has a total area of 540 square inches. Each patch has an area of 9 square inches. How much of the area of the quilt is white?

# Problem Solving

**6. Make Sense and Persevere** A ticket to a movie for a student is $7. The cost for an adult is $2 more than for a student. How much would it cost 5 adults and 29 students for tickets to the movie?

**7.** 🅰🅩 **Vocabulary** Give an example of an expression. Then give an example of an equation.

---

**8. Higher Order Thinking** Cody and Max both solve the problem below correctly. Explain how each solve.

Emma has $79 to spend at the toy store. She wants to buy a building set, a board game, and 2 action figures from her favorite movie. What else can she buy?

Cody
79 - 32 = 47
47 - 19 = 28
2 × 8 = 16
28 - 16 = 12

Emma can buy a doll or another action figure.

Max
L = the money Emma has left.
L = 79 - (32 + 19 + 16)
L = 79 - 67
L = 12

She can buy a doll or action figure.

| Toy Shop | |
|---|---|
| **Toy** | **Cost** |
| Building Set | $32 |
| Board Game | $19 |
| Stuffed Toy | $15 |
| Doll | $12 |
| Action Figure | $8 |

---

## Assessment Practice

**9.** A company has 2 geothermal plants which can power a total of 2,034 homes. After they build 3 additional, more powerful, geothermal plants, they can power a total of 5,799 homes. How many homes does each of the new plants power? Explain how you solve. Use one or more equations and bar diagrams in your explanation. Tell what your variables represent.

Activity

★ ☆ ★
Solve & Share

A farmer needs $3,500 to buy a previously-owned truck. If she sells 45 maple trees and 27 pine trees, will she earn enough to buy the truck? If not, how much more money does she need? *Solve this problem any way you choose.*

**I can ...**
solve multi-step problems by finding and solving hidden questions and by writing expressions and equations.

**I can also** reason about math to solve problems.

You can use reasoning and think about the relationships between the quantities in the problem.

Rothacker
**TREE FARM**
SALE!
Maple trees  $56
Pine trees  $33

**Look Back!** In the question above, how many more of each tree could the farmer sell to get enough money to buy the truck? Explain.

# How Can You Use Equations to Solve Multi-Step Problems?

**A**

*The students in the fourth and fifth grades are going to a concert. There are 178 students. How many rows are needed for the fourth graders?*

To find the number of rows, you need to find the number of fourth graders. To find the number of fourth graders, you need to find the number of fifth graders.

Each row has 8 seats.
The fifth-grade students fill 12 rows.

Let $s$ = the number of fifth graders, $f$ = the number of fourth graders, and $r$ = the number of rows of fourth graders.

**B** **Step 1**

Find and solve the first hidden question.

**Hidden Question:**
How many fifth graders are there?

$12 \times 8 = s$
$s = 96$

There are 96 fifth graders.

**C** **Step 2**

Find and solve the second hidden question.

**Hidden Question:**
How many fourth graders are there?

$178 - 96 = f$
$f = 82$

There are 82 fourth graders.

**D** **Step 3**

Answer the original question.

**Original Question:**
How many rows are needed for the fourth graders?

$82 \div 8 = r$
$r = 10$ R2

Ten rows will be filled with 2 fourth graders left over. So, 11 rows will be needed.

**Convince Me!** **Construct Arguments** Does the answer of 11 rows make sense for the problem above? Explain.

Practice  Tools  Assessment

# Guided Practice

## Do You Understand?

**1.** On the previous page, suppose there were only 11 rows of fifth graders, but the same total number of students. Do you need to solve the whole problem again to find how many rows are needed for the fourth graders? Explain.

## Do You Know How?

**2.** Show another way to solve the problem on the previous page.

# Independent Practice

For **3–4**, solve each multi-step problem. Write equations to show how you solve. Draw bar diagrams to help if needed. Use estimation to decide if your answer is reasonable.

**3.** Vanya bought 5 medium packages of buttons and 3 small packages of buttons. What was the total number of buttons Vanya bought?

**DATA**

### Number of Items in Package

| Item | Small | Medium | Large |
|------|-------|--------|-------|
| Beads | 32 | 64 | 96 |
| Buttons | 18 | 38 | 56 |

**4.** Vance bought 2 packages of large beads, 1 package of medium beads, 2 packages of large buttons, and 2 packages of medium buttons. How many more beads than buttons did Vance buy?

# Problem Solving

5. **enVision® STEM** How much more does it cost to generate 9 megawatt hours of electricity with conventional coal than with wind energy? Write one or more equations to show how you solve. Tell what your variables represent.

It can cost up to $87 to generate 1 megawatt hour of electricity with wind energy.

It can cost $105 to generate 1 megawatt hour of electricity with conventional coal.

6. **Model with Math** Anna earns $8 an hour baby-sitting and $6 an hour working in the garden. Last month, she worked 15 hours baby-sitting and 8 hours in the garden. How much more money does she need to buy a robot which costs $199? Explain how you solve. Use one or more equations in your explanation. Tell what your variables represent.

7. **Higher Order Thinking** Show two different ways to find the answer to the problem below.

Dog and cat food are sold in 20-pound bags. There are 14 bags of dog food and 12 bags of cat food on the store shelves. How many pounds of dog and cat food are on the shelves?

✓ **Assessment Practice**

8. Chris needs $858 to buy a computer. She has already saved $575. She gets $15 an hour for babysitting and will babysit 12 hours in the next month. She can save $8 a week from her allowance. How many weeks of allowance will it take Chris to save enough to buy the computer? Explain how you solve. Use one or more equations in your explanation. Tell what your variables represent.

Name _____

★ ★
**Solve & Share**

Ms. Valenzuela had her students design a snake house for the zoo. In the design shown, the anaconda has 538 more square feet than the python. The python has twice as many square feet as the rattlesnake. How much of the house's area does each snake have? *Solve this problem any way you choose.*

PYTHON
*p* square feet

RATTLESNAKE
*r* square feet

Viewing Area

ANACONDA
1,928 square feet

## Thinking Habits

*Be a good thinker! These questions can help you.*

• What do I need to find?

• What do I know?

• What's my plan for solving the problem?

• What else can I try if I get stuck?

• How can I check that my solution makes sense?

**Look Back!** **Make Sense and Persevere** How can you check that your solution makes sense?

Essential Question: **How Do You Make Sense of a Multi-Step Problem and Persevere in Solving It?**

**A**

*Bryan and Alex have to buy their own instruments for the band. Alex made $1,025 from a fundraiser. He has a part-time job that pays $8 an hour. How many hours does Alex need to work to have enough money to buy his instrument?*

Bryan's trumpet costs $159.

Alex's tuba costs 9 times as much as Bryan's trumpet.

### What do you need to do to solve this problem?

I need to determine how much Alex's tuba costs and how much Alex needs to earn to buy the tuba.

Here's my thinking.

**B** **How can I make sense of and solve this problem?**

**I can**

- identify the quantities given.

- understand how the quantities are related.

- choose and implement an appropriate strategy.

- check to be sure my work and answer make sense.

**C** Use the cost of the trumpet to find the cost of the tuba.

$159 × 9 = $1,431    Alex's tuba costs $1,431.

Find how much more money Alex needs to earn.

$1,431 − $1,025 = $406    Alex needs to earn $406.

Find how many hours Alex needs to work.

$406 ÷ 8 = 50 R6

Alex will not have enough money by working 50 hours, so he needs to work 51 hours.

**Convince Me!** **Make Sense and Persevere** How can you check to make sure the work and answer given above make sense?

# Guided Practice

**Make Sense and Persevere**

In the problem on the previous page, suppose Alex wanted to know how many weeks it would take him to work 51 hours. Alex works 3 hours a day and 4 days a week.

1. What are you asked to find and what is the hidden question?

2. Write and solve equations to solve the problem. Be sure to tell what each variable represents.

3. Does your answer make sense? Explain.

Think about this question to help you persevere in solving the problem. What's a good plan for solving the problem?

# Independent Practice

**Make Sense and Persevere**

The high school tennis team is selling tennis balls to raise $500 for new equipment. They sell the balls for $2 each. Will they make enough money if they sell 4 cases?

4. What are the hidden questions? Write equations to solve each.

A case has 24 packages.
Each package has 3 tennis balls.

5. Will the team make enough money? Explain.

# Problem Solving

## Designing a Flag

Rainey's group designed the flag shown for a class project. They used 234 square inches of green fabric. After making one flag, Rainey's group has 35 square inches of yellow fabric left. How can Rainey's group determine the total area of the flag?

Twice as much green as orange

3 times as much green as yellow

6. **Make Sense and Persevere** What hidden question(s) do you need to answer first?

7. **Appropriate Tools** Draw diagrams and write equations to represent the hidden question(s). Be sure to tell what each variable represents.

When you make sense of a problem, you check that your solution makes sense.

8. **Be Precise** Use your drawings and equations to find the total area of the flag. Explain carefully, using the correct units.

9. **Make Sense and Persevere** What information was not needed to solve the problem?

**Find a Match**

Work with a partner. Point to a clue.

Read the clue.

Look below the clues to find a match. Write the clue letter in the box next to the match.

Find a match for every clue.

**I can ...**
subtract multi-digit whole numbers.

**I can also** make math arguments.

**Clues**

**A** The difference is exactly 528.

**B** The difference is between 550 and 560.

**C** The difference is between 800 and 900.

**D** The difference is exactly 614.

**E** The difference is between 100 and 105.

**F** The difference is between 470 and 480.

**G** The difference is exactly 392.

**H** The difference is between 70 and 80.

| 917<br>− 365 | 994<br>− 137 | 647<br>− 574 | 792<br>− 178 |

| 653<br>− 125 | 865<br>− 394 | 947<br>− 555 | 552<br>− 448 |

# Vocabulary Review

A-Z
Glossary

## Word List

- addition comparison
- Associative Property of Multiplication
- Commutative Property of Multiplication
- Distributive Property of Multiplication
- equation
- multiplication comparison
- product
- variable

## Understand Vocabulary

Write T for *true* and F for *false*.

1. _____ Addition comparison is used when you can multiply to find how one quantity is related to another.

2. _____ Multiplication comparison is used when one quantity is *x* times more than another quantity.

3. _____ A number sentence that uses an equal sign to show that two expressions have the same value is called an equation.

4. _____ The answer to a subtraction problem is called the product.

5. _____ A symbol or letter that stands for a number is called a variable.

Label each example with a term from the Word List.

6. $(3 \times 4) \times 5 = 3 \times (4 \times 5)$    _____

7. $3 \times (4 + 5) = (3 \times 4) + (3 \times 5)$    _____

8. $3 \times 4 \times 5 = 4 \times 3 \times 5$    _____

## Use Vocabulary in Writing

9. Seth wrote and solved the following comparison:

   Find 6 times as many as 5.

   $6 \times 5 = n$
   $n = 30$

   Use at least 3 terms from the Word List to describe Seth's comparison.

**Set A** pages 225–232

Write an equation for each comparison. Find the value of the variable that makes the equation true.

$k$ is 9 times as many as 3.

$k = 9 \times 3$     $k = 27$

$m$ is 6 more than 21.

$m = 6 + 21$     $m = 27$

There are 30 apples and 6 bananas in a basket. How many times as many apples as bananas are in the basket?

Let $t$ = the number of times as many apples as bananas.

$t$ times as many as 6 is 30.

$t \times 6 = 30$

Since $5 \times 6 = 30$, there are 5 times as many apples as bananas in the basket.

**Remember** to use addition or subtraction when you know how much more, and multiplication or division when you know how many times as many.

**Reteaching**

Write and solve an equation to match each comparison.

1. $x$ is 21 more than 21.

2. Macon has 32 rocks in his collection. He has 4 times as many rocks as his brother. How many rocks, $r$, does Macon's brother have?

3. Pam has 24 pencils and 6 erasers. How many times, $t$, as many pencils as erasers does Pam have?

**Set B** pages 233–240

At a restaurant, a children's meal costs $5, and an adult meal costs $9. Four children and 2 adults order meals. The family has a $25 gift certificate to use. How much will their total be before tax?

$T$ = total cost of meals

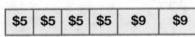

| $5 | $5 | $5 | $5 | $9 | $9 |

$4 \times \$5 = \$20$      $2 \times \$9 = \$18$
$T = \$20 + \$18$
$T = \$38$

*How much did the meals cost?*

$T$

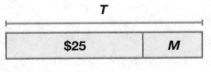

| $25 | M |

*Using the gift certificate, how much is the total?*

$\$38 - \$25 = M$
$M = \$13$

**Remember** to first find and answer any hidden questions.

1. There are 64 singers in the choir. The tenors and sopranos are in separate rows. There are 8 singers in each row. There are 4 rows of tenors. How many rows of sopranos are there?

2. Samantha has $600 saved for a trip. She buys an airline ticket for $120 and reserves a hotel room for $55 each night for 4 nights. If Samantha's trip lasts for 5 days and she spends the same amount each day, how much can Samantha spend each day?

There are 13 girls and 14 boys signed up to join volleyball. Each team needs 6 players. How many teams can be formed, and how many more players are needed to form one more team?

Find the total number of players signed up.

$13 + 14 = p$
$\quad\quad 27 = p$

Divide to find the number of teams that can be formed.

$27 \div 6 = t$
$\quad 4\ R3 = t$

There are 3 students left not on a team. Subtract to find the number of players still needed to make a team.

$6 - 3 = p$
$\quad\quad 3 = p$

4 teams can be formed. 3 more players are needed to make one more team.

**Remember** to draw bar diagrams to help if needed.

Solve each multi-step problem. Write equations to show how you solve.

1. Keiva made $96 in necklace sales and half that amount in bracelet sales. How much money did Keiva make in necklace and bracelet sales?

2. A dog and cat rescue uses 40 pounds of dog food and 15 pounds of cat food to feed its animals each day. How many pounds of dog and cat food do they use in seven days?

Think about these questions to help you **make sense** of the problem.

### Thinking Habits

- What do I need to find?

- What do I know?

- What's my plan for solving the problem?

- What else can I try if I get stuck?

- How can I check that my solution makes sense?

**Remember** to make sense of the problem before starting to solve it.

At a local shelter, each large dog can be adopted for $10 and each small dog for $5. There are 17 large dogs up for adoption. If all the dogs are adopted, the shelter will make $215. How many small dogs were at the shelter?

1. Find the hidden questions. Write equations to solve each.

2. How many small dogs are at the shelter?

**1.** Jason and his 3 brothers want to buy a gift for their mother. They have $314 saved. Each of them will save $17 a week until they have at least $515 for her gift. How much money will they save after 3 weeks? Will they have enough money to buy the gift?

**A.** What are the hidden questions?

**B.** Write an equation that can be used to answer each hidden question. Then solve.

**C.** Write and solve an equation to find how much money they will save after 3 weeks. Will they have enough to buy the gift? Explain.

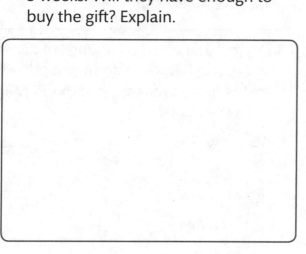

**2.** Marco ordered 2 reclining chairs for $230 each and a coffee table for $350. The shipping cost is $100. Marco is going to pay off his bill in 5 equal payments. How much is each of Marco's payments?

**3.** Mitchell wants to beat the record for the most points scored in a season. This season, he has scored 51 points. If he scores 27 points at each of the next 7 games, he will break the record by 1 point. How many total points will break the record by 1 point?

p points needed

| 27 | 27 | 27 | 27 | 27 | 27 | 27 |

☐ × 27 = p          p = ☐

m

| 51 | | ☐ |

☐ + 51 = m          m = ☐

Mitchell will break the record by 1 point if he scores a total of ☐ points.

**4.** Select all the sentences that describe a comparison using multiplication.

☐ 9 is 3 times as many as *p*.

☐ 27 more than *r* is 41.

☐ A bus can travel 3 times as fast as a boat.

☐ It costs *d* dollars for 9 packages.

☐ There are 4 times as many girls as boys.

**5.** Choose the correct word from the box to complete each statement.

| more than | times as many as |
|-----------|------------------|

45 is 9 [                    ] 5.

120 is 68 [                    ] 52.

86 is 12 [                    ] 74.

33 is 3 [                    ] 11.

**6.** Dee has $120 to spend. She went to the grocery store and spent $55. She then bought 3 potted flowers for $18 each at the nursery. How much money did Dee have left? Select each correct equation or set of equations that could be used to solve the question.

☐ $120 − $55 = M; M − (3 × $18)

☐ $120 − $55 − (3 × $18) = M

☐ (3 × $18) − $55 − $120 = M

☐ ($120 − $55) − (3 × $18) = M

☐ $120 + $55 − (3 × $18) = M

**7.** Darcy ordered 18 boxes of red balloons and 12 boxes of blue balloons for a party. She ordered a total of 240 balloons. How many balloons are in each box?

Ⓐ 6

Ⓑ 8

Ⓒ 7

Ⓓ 9

**8.** Select all of the sentences that are true for the number 9.

☐ 18 × __ = 162

☐ 20 more than __ = 180

☐ __ times as many as 16 is 145.

☐ 315 is __ times as many as 35.

☐ 16 × __ = 128

**9.** Select all the expressions that are equal to the product of 14 and 9.

☐ (2 × 7) + 9

☐ 9 times as many as 14

☐ 14 × 9

☐ 14 more than 9

☐ 9 less than 14

**10.** Maggie collected 63 pounds of paper for recycling. Carl collected 9 pounds. How many times as many pounds did Maggie collect as Carl?

Ⓐ 3 times

Ⓑ 5 times

Ⓒ 7 times

Ⓓ 8 times

## Ski Jumping

Jackie and her older brother Robert went skiing. The **Ski Jumping** table shows their best jumps, including the distance they jumped and the total length of their run.

| Ski Jumping | | |
|---|---|---|
| Distance | | |
| Feature | Robert | Jackie |
| Jump distance | 297 feet | 189 feet |
| Total length | 3 times the jump distance | 3 times the jump distance |

**1.** Jackie wants to find how much farther Robert's run was than her run.

### Part A

What is the total length of Robert's run? Draw a bar diagram and write and solve an equation to represent the problem. Does this situation use addition or multiplication to compare?

### Part B

How much farther was Robert's run than Jackie's run? Write equations to represent each step of the problem. Tell what your variables represent.

**2.** Jackie's run was the same on two different jumps. In the first, she jumped 145 feet and went an additional 167 feet after the jump. In the second, she jumped 135 feet. How many feet, *f*, did she go after the jump?

**3.** Use the **Beginner Jump** information to find how much longer the total length of the ski jump hill for an advanced jump is than a beginner jump. The advanced jump distance is 408 feet.

> **Beginner Jump**
>
> The advanced jump distance is 8 times the beginner jump distance.
>
> The total length of a beginner jump hill is 3 times the beginner jump distance.

**Part A**

What are the hidden questions you need to answer to solve the problem? Name a variable for each question.

**Part B**

How much longer is *d*, the total length of an advanced jump hill, than a beginner jump hill? Write equations and explain how to solve the hidden questions and the original question.

# Factors and Multiples

**Essential Questions:** How can you use arrays or multiplication to find the factors of a number? How can you identify prime and composite numbers? How can you find multiples of a number?

Animals have traits that allow them to survive in their habitats.

A penguins' dark feathers absorb heat from the sun to keep them warm in cold climates.

Penguins live in some of the coldest places on Earth! Here is a project on the animal kingdom and multiples.

**enVision** STEM **Project:** Analyzing the Animal Kingdom

**Do Research** As a defense against the cold, emperor penguins huddle together in large groups. Use the Internet or other sources to research how this helps them protect each other and their chicks.

**Journal: Write a Report** Include what you found. Also in your report:

• Suppose 64 penguins form a huddle to keep warm. Use a grid to draw all the possible arrays for 64.

• If a huddle of 72 penguins breaks apart, how many different ways can the penguins form equal groups? Is 72 prime or composite? Write the factor pairs of 72 to show all the ways the penguins can form equal groups.

# Review What You Know

## A-Z Vocabulary

Choose the best term from the box.
Write it on the blank.

| • dividend | • product |
| • divisor | • quotient |

1. The _____ is the answer to a division problem.

2. The number being divided is the _____.

3. The _____ is the number that tells into how many groups something is being divided.

## Multiplication

Find each product.

4. $8 \times 4$

5. $17 \times 6$

6. $304 \times 9$

7. $555 \times 5$

8. $22 \times 26$

9. $33 \times 11$

10. $56 \times 70$

11. $36 \times 91$

12. $27 \times 48$

13. $56 \times 13$

14. $12 \times 19$

15. $36 \times 16$

## Division

Find each quotient.

16. $27 \div 3$

17. $56 \div 8$

18. $36 \div 4$

19. $72 \div 9$

20. $39 \div 3$

21. $64 \div 4$

22. $105 \div 5$

23. $824 \div 4$

24. $942 \div 3$

25. $9,156 \div 3$

26. $2,156 \div 4$

27. $4,136 \div 8$

## Problem Solving

28. **Model with Math** Cecilia bought 2 sandwiches last week and 4 sandwiches this week. She spent a total of $42. If each sandwich costs the same amount, how much did Cecilia spend on each sandwich? Write and solve equations.

Name_____

### PROJECT 7A

**Where is Mammoth Cave National Park?**

**Project:** Model a Campground

### PROJECT 7B

**How many people can fill a college basketball arena?**

**Project:** Create a Basketball Arena

### PROJECT 7C

**How many arrays of potted plants do you see?**

**Project:** Design a Plant Array for a Store Display

Before watching the video, think:

People who work in a grocery store do many different jobs. Some employees make stacks of things for people to buy. Some employees clean up messes when people drop jars of tomato sauce. If an employee made a stack of jars, probably another employee would come around soon to clean up the mess.

**I can ...**

model with math to solve a problem that involves estimating and using factors and multiples.

Name _____

**Solve & Share**

Fourth graders at Ames School have 24 carpet squares. What are all the different ways they can organize the carpet squares into a rectangular array? **Solve this problem any way you choose.**

You can use grid paper or tiles, to find all the possible arrays.

**I can ...**
find the factor pairs of a whole number.

**I can also** look for patterns to solve problems.

**Look Back!** **Look for Relationships** What patterns do you see in the arrays?

**Essential Question**

# How Can You Use Arrays to Find the Factor Pairs of a Number?

**A**

The music director is trying to find the best way to arrange the chairs for a performance. The chairs must be arranged in a rectangular array. How many different ways can the chairs be arranged into a rectangular array? Use grids to show all the ways the chairs can be arranged.

Pairs of whole numbers multiplied together to find a product are called factor pairs. Think about multiplication to decompose a number into its factors.

12 chairs

**B** 1 row of 12 chairs
12 rows of 1 chair

$1 \times 12$

$12 \times 1$

1 and 12 are a factor pair.

**C** 2 rows of 6 chairs
6 rows of 2 chairs

$2 \times 6$

$6 \times 2$

2 and 6 are a factor pair.

**D** 3 rows of 4 chairs
4 rows of 3 chairs

$3 \times 4$

$4 \times 3$

3 and 4 are a factor pair.

There are 6 possible ways the 12 chairs can be arranged.

**Convince Me!** **Critique Reasoning** Blake says, "Greater numbers will always have more factors." Do you agree? Explain.

Name _____

# ☆ Guided Practice

## Do You Understand?

**1.** How are the lengths of the sides of the arrays shown on the grids on the previous page related to the factors of 12?

**2.** What are the lengths of the sides of the arrays that show how 5 chairs can be arranged?

## Do You Know How?

For **3–4**, find all of the factor pairs for each number. You can use grids to help.

**3.** 6                **4.** 16

For **5–6**, find the factors of each number.

**5.** 45               **6.** 30

# Independent Practice ☆

For **7–8**, use the grids to find all the possible arrays for each number. Use the arrays to help write the factors.

**7.** 9

**8.** 14

For **9–14**, use grids to find the factor pair or pairs for each number.

**9.** 5                          **10.** 25

**11.** 8                          **12.** 36

**13.** 23                         **14.** 27

# Problem Solving

**15. Reasoning** Use the grid to find two numbers that have 2 and 3 as factors.

Draw arrays with side lengths that have 2 and 3 as factors.

---

**16.** The dwarf planet Pluto takes about 90,403 days to orbit the sun. Write this number in expanded form and using number names.

**17.** David makes 17 dollars in an hour and works 25 hours each week. Linda makes 25 dollars in an hour and works 17 hours each week. How much do David and Linda make together each week? What property of multiplication does this represent?

---

**18.** What do you notice about the number of possible arrays and the number of factors of 22?

**19. Higher Order Thinking** Jane says 5 is a factor of every whole number that has a 5 in the ones place. Fred says 5 is a factor of every whole number that has a 0 in the ones place. Who is correct? Explain.

---

### ✓ Assessment Practice

**20.** Which of the following are factors of both 18 and 42? Select all that apply.

- ☐ 1
- ☐ 3
- ☐ 4
- ☐ 6
- ☐ 14

**21.** Which of the numbers below have 2, 3, and 4 as factors? Select all that apply.

- ☐ 86
- ☐ 72
- ☐ 36
- ☐ 32
- ☐ 24

Name_____

Activity

☆ ☆
**Solve & Share**

Jared has 20 flowers. He wants to plant all of the flowers in equal rows in his garden. What are the different ways Jared can arrange the flowers in equal rows? *Solve this problem any way you choose.*

**I can ...**
use multiplication to find the factor pairs for a whole number.

**I can also** make sense of problems.

You can use what you know about multiplying whole numbers to find equal rows.

**Look Back!** **Make Sense and Persevere** How can you check you have found all the different ways Jared can plant his flowers?

**Essential Question** **How Can You Use Multiplication to Find the Factors of a Number?**

**A**

Jean wants to arrange her action figures in equal-size groups. What are all the ways Jean can arrange her action figures?

Jean can think of all the factor pairs of 16. Factor pairs are two whole numbers that when multiplied give you a certain product.

16 action figures

**B** 1 group of 16

16 groups of 1

Jean can arrange 1 group of 16 figures or 16 groups of 1 figure.

$1 \times 16 = 16$
$16 \times 1 = 16$

So, 1 and 16 are factors of 16.

**C** 8 groups of 2

2 groups of 8

Jean can arrange 8 groups of 2 figures or 2 groups of 8 figures.

$2 \times 8 = 16$
$8 \times 2 = 16$

So, 2 and 8 are factors of 16.

**D** 4 groups of 4

Jean can arrange 4 groups of 4 figures. 4 is a factor of 16.

$4 \times 4 = 16$

The factor pairs for 16 are 1 and 16, 2 and 8, and 4 and 4.

**Convince Me!** **Construct Arguments** How do you know there are no other factors for 16 other than 1, 2, 4, 8, and 16? Explain.

Practice  Tools  Assessment

# ☆ Guided Practice

## Do You Understand?

**1.** Jean bought 7 more action figures. What are the different equal-size groups she can make now?

**2.** What factor besides 1 does every even number have?

## Do You Know How?

For **3–6**, write the factors of each number. Use counters to help.

**3.** 2                **4.** 20

**5.** 28               **6.** 54

# ☆ Independent Practice ☆

Remember, the factors of a number always include 1 and the number.

**Leveled Practice** For **7–12**, write the factor pairs for each number.

**7.** 34
_____ and 34
2 and _____

**8.** 39
1 and _____
_____ and 13

**9.** 61
1 and _____

**10.** 14
_____ and _____
_____ and _____

**11.** 22
_____ and _____
_____ and _____

**12.** 51
_____ and _____
_____ and _____

For **13–21**, write the factors of each number. Use counters to help as needed.

**13.** 6

**14.** 32

**15.** 83

**16.** 11

**17.** 49

**18.** 25

**19.** 30

**20.** 63

**21.** 19

# Problem Solving

**22.** Irene wants to list the factors for 88. She writes 2, 4, 8, 11, 22, 44, and 88. Is Irene correct? Explain.

**23. enVision®** STEM  The roots of a plant are often the largest part of the plant. Winter rye can grow combined root tissue well over 984,000 feet in length. Write this number in expanded form.

**24. Model with Math**  A restaurant receives a shipment of 5,000 ketchup packets. In one week, they use 1,824 packets. The next week, they use 2,352 packets. Write and solve equations to find how many ketchup packets the restaurant has left.

**25.** Any number that has 9 as a factor also has 3 as a factor. Why is this?

**26. Higher Order Thinking**  A mother manatee, pictured to the right, is three times as long as her baby manatee.

   **a.** How long is her baby manatee? Write and solve an equation.

   **b.** If a blue whale is 9 times as long as the manatee shown, how much longer is a blue whale than the manatee? Write and solve equations.

12 feet

**27.** Which number has 3 and 29 as one of its factor pairs?

   Ⓐ  3

   Ⓑ  17

   Ⓒ  67

   Ⓓ  87

**28.** A store manager wants to display 45 cans of soup in an array. Which of the following shows 3 ways the cans could be displayed?

   Ⓐ  $1 \times 9, 9 \times 5, 3 \times 15$

   Ⓑ  $15 \times 3, 9 \times 1, 5 \times 9$

   Ⓒ  $5 \times 9, 3 \times 15, 9 \times 5$

   Ⓓ  $45 \times 1, 15 \times 1, 9 \times 1$

Name _____

**Solve & Share**

A closet company sells wooden storage cubicles. Jane bought 24 cubicles. She wants to arrange them in a rectangular array. What are all of the different ways Jane can arrange them, using all of her cubicles? Explain how you know you found them all.

**I can ...**
use repeated reasoning to generalize how to solve similar problems.

**I can also** use the Commutative Property of Multiplication to solve problems.

DATA

| These cubicles are arranged in an array. | These cubicles are not arranged in an array. |
|---|---|
|  |  |

## Thinking Habits

*Be a good thinker! These questions can help you.*

- Are any calculations repeated?

- Can I generalize from examples?

- What shortcuts do I notice?

**Look Back!** **Generalize** Do you need to try all numbers from 1 to 24 to be sure you have all the factor pairs for 24? Explain.

**Essential Question** **How Can You Use Repeated Reasoning to Find All the Factors for a Number?**

**A**

A new city park is opening. The gardener needs to select 15 trees from a nursery and plant the trees in a rectangular array. What are all the different ways the gardener can plant the trees?

**Can you look for a general method to solve this problem?**

I can find all the possible factors of 15 that can be arranged in a rectangular array.

Select 15 trees to plant

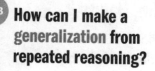

Here's my thinking.

**B** **How can I make a generalization from repeated reasoning?**

**I can**

- look for things that repeat in a problem.

- look for shortcuts.

- generalize from the example.

**C** To find all of the factors of 15, I divide **15** by divisors starting with 1. Then I use the Commutative Property to write two multiplication equations.

$1 \times 15 = 15$ and $15 \times 1 = 15$
2 is not a factor
$3 \times 5 = 15$ and $5 \times 3 = 15$
4 is not a factor
$5 \times 3 = 15$ and $3 \times 5 = 15$

I already found the factor paired with 5, $3 \times 5$ and $5 \times 3$.

When factor pairs start repeating, you can make a general statement, or generalize, that all the factors of a number are found.

The gardener has 4 different ways to plant the trees: $1 \times 15$, $15 \times 1$, $5 \times 3$, and $3 \times 5$ arrays.

**Convince Me!** **Construct Arguments** The diagram shows all the factor pairs of 24. Use the diagram to justify the conclusion that when factor pairs start repeating, you know you have found all the factors of a number.

Name_____

# ☆ Guided Practice

**Generalize**

Ms. Maribel wants to arrange the 20 desks in her classroom into rows with the same number of desks in each row. She wants at least 2, but not more than 8 rows.

When you generalize, you find general methods and shortcuts to help solve a problem.

1. What are the factor pairs for 20? Explain how you know you have found them all.

2. Find the ways Ms. Maribel can arrange the desks.

# Independent Practice ☆

**Generalize**

Kevin invited 15 friends to his birthday party. They played a game where everyone had to separate into groups. Each group had the same number of children. The game could not be played with all 16 children in one group and each group had to have more than 1 child.

3. List the factor pairs of 16 and then find the different ways Kevin and his friends could divide into groups.

4. Why does 16 have an odd number of factors?

5. Can you stop checking for factor pairs when you find a pair that repeats? Explain.

# Problem Solving

## Store Displays

A pet store needs 3 displays with the products shown. The boxes of kitty litter need to be stacked with the same number of boxes in each row. There needs to be at least 3 rows with at least 3 boxes in each row. What are all the ways the boxes of kitty litter could be stacked?

50 fish bowls

48 boxes of kitty litter

88 bags of dog food

6. **Make Sense and Persevere** What quantities are given in the problem and what do the numbers mean?

When you notice repetition in calculations, you can generalize to help solve problems.

7. **Reasoning** What are the factor pairs for 48?

8. **Be Precise** What are all the ways the boxes of kitty litter can be stacked with at least 3 rows with at least 3 boxes in each row?

Name_____

## Solve & Share

Max has 2 red tiles, 3 blue tiles, 4 yellow tiles, and 8 green tiles. How many different rectangular arrays of each color can Max make? Explain how you know you found all the arrays. **Solve this problem any way you choose.**

**I can ...**
use factors to determine if a whole number is prime or composite.

**I can also** reason about math.

You can use reasoning. Find the factors of each number of tiles to help find the number of arrays.

**Look Back!** What do you notice about the factors of each number of color tiles and the number of arrays?

**Essential Question**

# How Can You Identify Prime and Composite Numbers?

**A**

The data table lists the factors for 2, 3, 4, 5, and 6. What do you notice about the factors for 5? What do you notice about the factors for 6?

**DATA**

| Number | Factors |
|--------|---------|
| 2 | 1, 2 |
| 3 | 1, 3 |
| 4 | 1, 2, 4 |
| 5 | 1, 5 |
| 6 | 1, 2, 3, 6 |

A prime number is a whole number greater than 1 that has exactly two factors, 1 and itself.

A composite number is a whole number greater than 1 that has more than 2 factors.

**B** **Prime Numbers**

5 is a prime number.
It has only 2 factors, 1 and itself.

$1 \times 5 = 5$         $5 \times 1 = 5$

The number 1 is a special number. It is neither prime nor composite.

**C** **Composite Numbers**

6 is a composite number.
The factors for 6 are 1, 2, 3, and 6.

$1 \times 6 = 6$         $6 \times 1 = 6$

$2 \times 3 = 6$        $3 \times 2 = 6$

**Convince Me!** **Generalize** Can a number be both prime and composite? Explain.

#  Guided Practice

## Do You Understand?

**1.** What is the only even prime number?

**2.** Write an odd number that is not prime. What makes it a composite number?

**3.** Roger has 47 cars. Can he group the cars in more than 2 ways?

## Do You Know How?

For **4–9**, tell whether each number is prime or composite.

**4.** 32          **5.** 51

**6.** 73          **7.** 21

**8.** 95          **9.** 29

A number is composite if it has more than 2 factors.

# Independent Practice

**Leveled Practice** For **10–19**, tell whether each number is prime or composite.

**10.** 7

**11.** 10

**12.** 12          **13.** 97          **14.** 90          **15.** 31

**16.** 11          **17.** 44          **18.** 3          **19.** 59

# Problem Solving

For **20–21**, use the graph at the right.

**20.** Which type of flower received a prime number of votes?

**21.** How many votes are represented by the picture graph?

**Favorite Flowers**

| | |
|---|---|
| Daffodils | |
| Daisies | |
| Tulips | |

Key: Each flower icon equals 2 votes.

---

**22.** **Critique Reasoning** Maria says every number in the nineties is composite. Jackie says 1 number in the nineties is prime. Who is correct? Explain your answer.

**23.** **Critique Reasoning** Greta says the product of two prime numbers must also be prime. Joan disagreed. Who is correct?

---

**24.** Janelle has 342 pennies, 62 nickels, and 12 dimes. If Janelle exchanges her coins for dollars, how many dollars will she have? How many cents will remain?

**25.** **Higher Order Thinking** Why is 1 neither a prime number nor a composite number?

---

## Assessment Practice

**26.** Select all the groups of numbers that are prime.

- ☐ 17, 19, 53
- ☐ 37, 43, 79
- ☐ 52, 67, 99
- ☐ 63, 72, 83
- ☐ 59, 89, 97

**27.** Select all the expressions with sums that are composite.

- ☐ 17 + 25
- ☐ 33 + 51
- ☐ 16 + 83
- ☐ 29 + 32
- ☐ 47 + 29

**276** **Topic 7** | Lesson 7-4

**I can ...**
use multiplication to find multiples
of a number.

**I can also** reason about math.

☆ ☆
**Solve & Share**

There are 9 players on the golf practice range.
If each player practices with the same number of golf
balls, how many balls might be in play at the same time?
**Solve this problem any way you choose.**

You can use reasoning.
What do you notice about the
number of balls in play?

| Golf Balls in Play | |
|---|---|
| **Balls per Player** | **Balls in Play** |
| 1 | $1 \times 9 = 9$ balls in play |
| 2 | $2 \times 9 = 18$ balls in play |
| 3 | $3 \times 9 = 27$ balls in play |
| 4 | |
| 5 | |

**Look Back!** Can you show all of the answers for the
problem? Explain.

**Essential Question**

# How Can You Find Multiples of a Number?

**A**

It takes 8 minutes for Car A to make one full turn on the Ferris wheel. If the Ferris wheel continues to turn at the same speed for the next hour, at what times during the hour will Car A return to the starting point?

A **multiple** is the product of a given factor and a whole number.

Starting point

---

**B** ## Step 1

One full turn takes 8 minutes.

$$1 \times 8 = 8$$

8 is a multiple of 1 and 8 because $1 \times 8 = 8$.

Car A is back at the starting point after 8 minutes.

**C** ## Step 2

Two full turns take 16 minutes.

$$2 \times 8 = 16$$

Car A is back at the starting point after another 8 minutes.

2 and 8 are factors of 16. 16 is a multiple of 2 and 8.

**D** ## Step 3

Car A is at the starting point every 8 minutes after that:

$$3 \times 8 = 24$$
$$4 \times 8 = 32$$
$$5 \times 8 = 40$$
$$6 \times 8 = 48$$
$$7 \times 8 = 56$$

During the hour, Car A returns to the starting point after 8, 16, 24, 32, 40, 48, and 56 minutes.

---

**Convince Me!** **Reasoning** What is the next multiple after 56? Explain why it is **NOT** used.

## Another Example!

Factors are numbers that when multiplied together give a product.
A whole number is a multiple of each of its factors.

Factors of 24 are 1, 2, 3, 4, 6, 8, 12, and 24.
24 is a multiple of 1, 2, 3, 4, 6, 8, 12, and 24.

## ☆ Guided Practice

### Do You Understand?

1. If the Ferris wheel in the example on the previous page turns at the same speed, will Car A return to the starting point at 75 minutes? Explain.

2. Suppose the Ferris wheel speeds up so it makes one full turn every 6 minutes. When will Car A return to the starting point if the Ferris wheel continues to turn for one half hour?

### Do You Know How?

For **3–4**, write five multiples of each number.

**3.** 2                    **4.** 9

For **5–6**, tell whether the first number is a multiple of the second number.

**5.** 14, 2                **6.** 3, 18

## Independent Practice ☆

For **7–14**, write five multiples of each number.

You can skip count to find multiples of numbers. Be Precise.

**7.** 7          **8.** 4          **9.** 6          **10.** 5

**11.** 11        **12.** 1         **13.** 20         **14.** 15

For **15–18**, tell whether the first number is a multiple of the second number.

**15.** 44, 6        **16.** 25, 5        **17.** 30, 6        **18.** 54, 9

# Problem Solving

**19.** Name all the numbers of which 45 is a multiple.

**20. Critique Reasoning** Lindsay says all numbers that are multiples of 4 have 2 as a factor. Is Lindsay correct? Explain.

**21.** Trisha bought bags of tennis balls. There are eight tennis balls in each bag. Could Trisha have 75 tennis balls? Explain.

**22. Higher Order Thinking** Gerri says that if a number is a multiple of 9 it is also a multiple of 3. Do you agree? Explain.

**23.** Describe how 20,000 and 2,000 are related.

**24.** Isabel wrote this mystery problem: The quotient is a multiple of 6. The dividend is a multiple of 9. The divisor is a factor of 12. Write one possible equation to Isabel's mystery problem.

## ✓ Assessment Practice

**25.** Latifa and John played a game of multiples. Each player picks a number card and says a multiple of that number. Latifa picked a 9. Write all the multiples of 9 from the box.

| 9 | 17 | 29 |
|---|----|----|
| 36 | 45 | 51 |

Multiples of 9

**26.** A roller-coaster ride completes a full loop every 3 minutes. Seth listed multiples of 3 to determine when the ride would be back at its starting point. Write all the multiples of 3 from the box.

| 9 | 11 | 12 |
|---|----|----|
| 13 | 19 | 33 |

Multiples of 3

Shade a path from **START** to **FINISH**. Follow the sums and differences that are correct. You can only move up, down, right, or left.

**I can ...**
add and subtract multi-digit whole numbers.

**I can also** be precise in my work.

| Start | | | | |
|---|---|---|---|---|
| 573<br>+ 417<br>**990** | 685<br>− 559<br>**137** | 808<br>+ 123<br>**921** | 609<br>− 541<br>**48** | 501<br>+ 469<br>**170** |
| 491<br>− 188<br>**303** | 347<br>+ 607<br>**954** | 948<br>− 558<br>**410** | 505<br>+ 125<br>**620** | 987<br>− 696<br>**311** |
| 764<br>+ 346<br>**1,000** | 994<br>− 405<br>**589** | 874<br>+ 721<br>**1,595** | 894<br>− 455<br>**449** | 369<br>+ 290<br>**669** |
| 668<br>− 485<br>**253** | 762<br>+ 901<br>**2,663** | 941<br>− 725<br>**216** | 640<br>+ 89<br>**729** | 537<br>− 271<br>**806** |
| 119<br>+ 679<br>**698** | 977<br>− 239<br>**642** | 987<br>+ 111<br>**998** | 812<br>− 99<br>**713** | 335<br>+ 25<br>**360** |

Finish

# Vocabulary Review

 A-Z
Glossary

## Word List

- array
- composite number
- factor
- factor pairs
- generalization
- multiple
- prime number
- whole number

## Understand Vocabulary

**1.** Cross out the numbers that are **NOT** factors of 16.

1      2      3      4      8

**2.** Cross out the numbers that are **NOT** multiples of 3.

3      6      9      13      23

**3.** Cross out the numbers that are **NOT** whole numbers.

$\frac{1}{4}$      $\frac{1}{2}$      7      $17\frac{1}{5}$      6,219

**4.** Cross out the numbers that are **NOT** factor pairs for 24.

1 and 24      2 and 12      3 and 6      4 and 8      4 and 6

Label each example with a term from the Word List.

**5.** 13 _____

**6.** 12 _____

**7.** ●●● _____

**8.** When factor pairs begin repeating, _____
I have found all the pairs for a number.

## Use Vocabulary in Writing

**9.** Marisol says 23 is both a prime and a composite number because 2 and 3 are both prime. Use at least 3 terms from the Word List to explain the error in Marisol's reasoning.

### Set A | pages 261–264

Draw arrays to find all the factor pairs for 8.

1 × 8

2 × 4

8 × 1

4 × 2

1 row of 8
8 rows of 1

2 rows of 4
4 rows of 2

The factor pairs for 8 are 1 and 8, 2 and 4.

**Remember** that 1 is a factor of every number.

Use grid paper to find the factor pairs for each number.

1. 26

2. 9

3. 37

4. 24

5. 19

### Set B | pages 265–268

Find the factor pairs for 12.

1 and 12
2 and 6
3 and 4

The factors of 12 are 1, 2, 3, 4, 6, and 12.

**Remember** you can use counters or grids to make arrays and find the factors of a number.

Find the factors of each number.

1. 45

2. 40

3. 56

4. 63

### Set C | pages 269–272

Think about these questions to help you use **repeated reasoning**.

**Thinking Habits**

• Are any calculations repeated?

• Can I generalize from examples?

• What shortcuts do I notice?

**Remember** to look for repeating factors when dividing to find the factor pairs of a number.

A valet has 34 cars to park in a rectangular array.

1. What are the different ways the valet could park the cars?

2. How do you know when you can stop looking for factors of a number?

Is 49 prime or composite?

To determine if 49 is prime or composite, find whether 49 has factors other than 1 and 49.

49 is composite because it is divisible by 7.

$49 = 7 \times 7$

**Remember** you can use an array to determine if a number is prime or composite.

Tell whether each number is prime or composite.

1. 13

2. 25

3. 55

4. 2

5. 29

6. 23

7. 64

8. 99

9. 5

10. 21

Find five multiples of 7.

Use multiplication.

$7 \times 1 = 7$

$7 \times 2 = 14$

$7 \times 3 = 21$

$7 \times 4 = 28$

$7 \times 5 = 35$

You can skip count to find multiples of a number.

**Remember** that to find multiples of a number, multiply the number by any whole number.

Find five multiples of each number.

1. 3

2. 6

3. 4

4. 9

Tell whether the first number is a multiple of the second number.

5. 22, 2

6. 29, 3

7. 25, 5

8. 40, 8

Name_____

## Arranging Cars to Sell

Ms. Ortiz owns a car dealership. The dealership has the inventory of cars listed in the **Ortiz Car Dealership** table.

1. Ms. Ortiz wants to arrange all of the trucks in the front lot. She would like to have same number of trucks in each row.

### Part A

How many different ways can the trucks be arranged in the front lot if the same number of trucks are parked in each row?

| | Ortiz Car Dealership | |
|---|---|---|
| DATA | Type of Vehicle | Number Dealership Has |
| | Compact | 40 |
| | Sedan | 36 |
| | SUV | 23 |
| | Truck | 15 |

### Part B

What are all the ways the trucks can be arranged? Draw and label the different arrays.

### Part C

Ms. Ortiz would like the arrangement to have more than 2 rows of trucks but less than 6 rows. What are the ways the trucks can be arranged? Explain.

**2.** As Ms. Ortiz sells sedans, those sedans remaining are parked in different arrangements.

Complete the **Arranging Sedans** table to find the number of ways Ms. Ortiz can arrange each number of sedans in the front lot so there are at least 2 rows with the same number of sedans in each row and more than one sedan in each row.

Arranging Sedans

| Sedans Sold | Number Left | Number of Arrangements | Arrangements |
|---|---|---|---|
| 1 | | | |
| 2 | | | |
| 3 | | | |
| 4 | | | |
| 5 | | | |
| 6 | | | |
| 7 | | | |

# Glossary

**acute angle** An angle that is open less than a right angle.

**acute triangle** A triangle that has three acute angles.

**addends** The numbers that are added together to find a sum.
*Example:* $2 + 7 = 9$

Addends

**algorithm** A set of steps used to solve a math problem.

**angle** A figure formed by two rays that have the same endpoint.

**angle measure** The number of degrees in an angle.

**area** The number of square units needed to cover a region.

**area model** A rectangle used to model multiplication and division of whole numbers.

**array** A way of displaying objects in rows and columns.

**Associative Property of Addition** Addends can be regrouped and the sum remains the same.

**Associative Property of Multiplication** Factors can be regrouped and the product stays the same.

B

**bar diagram** A tool used to help understand and solve word problems.

**bar graph** A graph using bars to show data.

**benchmark fraction** A known fraction that is commonly used for estimating.
*Examples:* $\frac{1}{4}$, $\frac{1}{3}$, $\frac{1}{2}$, $\frac{2}{3}$, and $\frac{3}{4}$

**billions** A period of three places to the left of the millions period.

**breaking apart** Mental math method used to rewrite a number as the sum of numbers to form an easier problem.

C

**capacity** The amount a container can hold, measured in liquid units.

**center** A point within a circle that is the same distance from all points on a circle.

**centimeter (cm)** A metric unit used to measure length. 100 centimeters = 1 meter

**century** A unit of time equal to 100 years.

**circle** A closed plane figure in which all the points are the same distance from a point called the center.

Circle
Center

**common denominator** A number that is the denominator of two or more fractions.

**common factor** A number that is a factor of two or more given numbers.

**Commutative Property of Addition** Numbers can be added in any order and the sum remains the same.

**Commutative Property of Multiplication** Factors can be multiplied in any order and the product stays the same.

**compare** Decide if one number is greater than, less than, or equal to another number.

**compatible numbers** Numbers that are easy to compute mentally.

**compensation** Choosing numbers close to the numbers in a problem to make the computation easier, and then adjusting the answer for the numbers chosen.

**compose** To combine parts.

**composite number** A whole number greater than 1 with more than two factors.

**conjecture** Statement that is believed to be true but has not been proven.

**count down** Counting down the lesser number from the greater number to find the difference of the two numbers.

**count up** Counting up from the lesser number to the greater number to find the difference of two numbers.

**cube** A solid figure with six identical squares as its faces.

**cubic unit** The volume of a cube that measures 1 unit on each edge.

**cup (c)** A customary unit of capacity. 1 cup = 8 fluid ounces

**customary units of measure** Units of measure that are used in the United States.

**data** Pieces of collected information.

**day** A unit of time equal to 24 hours.

**decade** A unit of time equal to 10 years.

**decimal** A number with one or more digits to the right of the decimal point.

**decimal point** A dot used to separate dollars from cents in money or to separate ones from tenths in a number.

**decimeter (dm)** A metric unit of length equal to 10 centimeters.

**decompose** To break into parts.

**degree (°)** A unit of measure for angles. $1° = \frac{1}{360}$ of a circle. Also a unit of measure for temperature.

**denominator** The number below the fraction bar in a fraction that represents the total number of equal parts in one whole.

**difference** The answer when subtracting two numbers.

**digits** The symbols used to write a number: 0, 1, 2, 3, 4, 5, 6, 7, 8, and 9.

**Distributive Property** Multiplying a sum (or difference) by a number is the same as multiplying each number in the sum (or difference) by that number and adding (or subtracting) the products. *Example:* $(3 \times 21) = (3 \times 20) + (3 \times 1)$

**divide** An operation to find the number in each group or the number of equal groups.

**dividend** The number to be divided.

**divisibility rules** The rules that state when a number is divisible by another number.

**divisible** Can be divided by another number without leaving a remainder. *Example:* 10 is divisible by 2

**divisor** The number by which another number is divided.
*Example:* $32 \div 4 = 8$
↑
Divisor

**dot plot** A type of line plot that uses dots to indicate the number of times a response occurred.

**elapsed time** The amount of time between the beginning of an event and the end of the event.

**equation** A number sentence that uses the equal sign ( = ) to show that two expressions have the same value. *Example:* $9 + 3 = 12$

**equilateral triangle** A triangle with three sides that are the same length.

**equivalent** Numbers that name the same amount.

**equivalent fractions** Fractions that name the same region, part of a set, or part of a segment.

**estimate** To give an approximate value rather than an exact answer.

**expanded form** A number written as the sum of the values of its digits. *Example:* 2,476 = 2,000 + 400 + 70 + 6

**expression** A mathematical phrase. *Examples: x* − 3 or 2 + 7

**fact family** A group of related facts using the same set of numbers.

**factor pairs** Numbers that when multiplied together give a certain product.

**factors** The numbers that are multiplied together to give a product. *Example:* 3 × 6 = 18

Factors

**fluid ounce (fl oz)** A customary unit of capacity. 1 fluid ounce = 2 tablespoons; 8 fluid ounces = 1 cup

**foot (ft)** A customary unit of length. 1 foot = 12 inches

**formula** An equation that uses symbols to relate two or more quantities. *Example: A* = ℓ × w

**fraction** A symbol, such as $\frac{2}{3}$, $\frac{5}{1}$, or $\frac{8}{5}$, used to name a part of a whole, a part of a set, or a location on a number line.

**frequency** The number of times that a response occurs in a set of data.

**frequency table** A way to display data that shows how many times a response occurs in a set of data.

**gallon (gal)** A customary unit of capacity. 1 gallon = 4 quarts

**generalize** To make a general statement.

**gram (g)** A metric unit of mass. 1,000 grams = 1 kilogram

**greater than symbol (>)** A symbol that points away from a greater number or expression. *Example:* 450 > 449

**hexagon** A polygon with 6 sides.

**hour** A unit of time equal to 60 minutes.

**hundredth** One part of 100 equal parts of a whole.

**Identity Property of Addition** The sum of any number and zero is that number.

**Identity Property of Multiplication** The product of any number and one is that number.

**inch (in.)** A customary unit of length.
12 inches = 1 foot

**inequality** A number sentence that uses the greater than sign (>) or the less than sign (<) to show that two expressions do not have the same value. *Example:* 5 > 3

**intersecting lines** Lines that pass through the same point.

**interval** A number which is the difference between two consecutive numbers on the scale of a graph.

**inverse operations** Operations that undo each other.
*Examples:* Adding 6 and subtracting 6; Multiplying by 4 and dividing by 4.

**isosceles triangle** A triangle with at least two equal sides.

**key** Part of a graph that tells what each symbol stands for.

**kilogram (kg)** A metric unit of mass equal to 1,000 grams. 1 kilogram = 1,000 grams

**kilometer (km)** A metric unit of length equal to 1,000 meters.
1 kilometer = 1,000 meters

**leap year** A calendar occurrence that happens every four years when an extra day is added to February. Leap years have 366 days.

**less than symbol (<)** A symbol that points towards a lesser number or expression. *Example:* 305 < 320

**line** A straight path of points that goes on and on in opposite directions.

**line of symmetry** A line on which a figure can be folded so both halves are the same.

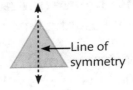

Line of symmetry

**line plot** A way to display data along a number line, where each dot or X represents one number in a set of data.

**line segment** A part of a line that has two endpoints.

**line symmetric** A figure that can be folded on a line to form two halves that fit exactly on top of each other.

**liter (L)** A metric unit of capacity.
1 liter = 1,000 milliliters

## M

**mass** The amount of matter that something contains.

**meter (m)** A metric unit of length. 1 meter = 100 centimeters

**metric units of measure** Units of measure commonly used by scientists.

**mile (mi)** A customary unit of length. 1 mile = 5,280 feet

**millennium (plural: millennia)** A unit for measuring time equal to 1,000 years.

**milligram (mg)** A metric unit of mass. 1,000 milligrams = 1 gram

**milliliter (mL)** A metric unit of capacity. 1,000 milliliters = 1 liter

**millimeter (mm)** A metric unit of length. 1,000 millimeters = 1 meter

**millions** In a number, a period of three places to the left of the thousands period.

**minute** A unit of time equal to 60 seconds.

**mixed number** A number that has a whole number part and a fraction part.

**month** One of the 12 parts into which a year is divided.

**multiple** The product of a given whole number and any non-zero whole number.

## N

**number name** A way to write a number in words. *Example:* Four thousand, six hundred thirty-two

**numerator** In a fraction, the number above the fraction bar that represents the part of the whole.

**numerical expression** An expression that contains numbers and at least one operation. *Example:* 35 + 12

## O

**obtuse angle** An angle that is open more than a right angle but less than a straight angle.

**obtuse triangle** A triangle that has one obtuse angle.

**octagon** A polygon with 8 sides.

**ounce (oz)** A customary unit of weight. 16 ounces = 1 pound

**overestimate** An estimate that is greater than the exact answer.

**P**

**parallel lines**
Lines that never intersect.

**parallelogram**
A quadrilateral that has
two pairs of parallel sides.

**partial products** Products found by
breaking one factor in a multiplication
problem into ones, tens, hundreds, and so
on and then multiplying each of these by
the other factor.

**partial quotients** A way to divide
that finds quotients in parts until only
a remainder, if any, is left.

**pentagon** A plane figure with 5 sides.

**perimeter** The distance around a figure.

**period** In a number, a group of three
digits, separated by commas, starting from
the right.

**perpendicular lines** Intersecting
lines that form right angles.

**pint (pt)** A customary unit of capacity.
1 pint = 2 cups

**place value** The value given to a place a
digit has in a number.
*Example:* In 3,946, the 9 is in the hundreds
place. So, the 9 has a value of 900.

**point** An exact location in space.

**polygon** A closed plane figure made up
of line segments.

**pound (lb)** A customary unit of weight.
1 pound = 16 ounces

**prime number** A whole number greater
than 1 that has exactly two factors, itself
and 1.

**product** The answer to a
multiplication problem.

**protractor** A tool used to measure and
draw angles.

**Q**

**quadrilateral** A polygon with 4 sides.

**quart (qt)** A customary unit of capacity.
1 quart = 2 pints

**quotient** The answer to a
division problem.

**R**

**ray** A part of a line that has one endpoint and continues on forever in one direction.

**rectangle** A quadrilateral that has four right angles.

**rectangular prism** A solid figure with 6 rectangular faces.

**regroup** To name a whole number in a different way. *Example:* 32 = 2 tens 12 ones

**remainder** The number that remains after the division is complete.

**repeated addition** A way to write a multiplication expression as an addition expression. *Example:* 3 × 5 = 5 + 5 + 5

**repeating pattern** Made up of shapes or numbers that form a part that repeats.

**rhombus** A quadrilateral that has opposite sides that are parallel and all of its sides are the same length.

**right angle** An angle that forms a square corner.

**right triangle** A triangle that has one right angle.

**rounding** A process that determines which multiple of 10, 100, 1,000, and so on a number is closest to.

**rule** A mathematical phrase that tells how numbers in a table are related.

**S**

**scale** Numbers that show the units used on a graph.

**scalene triangle** A triangle with no sides that are the same length.

**second** A unit of time. 60 seconds = 1 minute

**sequence** A set of numbers that follows a pattern.

**side** Each of the line segments of a polygon.

**solid figure** A figure with three dimensions that has length, width, and height.

**solution** The value of the variable that makes an equation true.

**solve an equation** Find a solution to an equation.

**square** A quadrilateral that has four right angles and all sides are the same length.

**square unit** A square with sides one unit long used to measure area.

**standard form** A way to write a number showing only its digits. Commas separate groups of three digits starting from the right. *Example:* 613,095

**straight angle** An angle that forms a straight line.

**sum** The result of adding numbers together.

**survey** Collecting information by asking a number of people the same question and recording their answers.

**tablespoon (tbsp)** A customary unit of capacity. 1 tablespoon = 3 teaspoons

**teaspoon (tsp)** A customary unit of capacity. 3 teaspoons = 1 tablespoon

**tenth** One part of 10 equal parts of a whole.

**terms** Numbers in a sequence or variables, such as *x* and *y*, in an expression.

**ton (T)** A customary unit of weight. 1 ton = 2,000 pounds

**trapezoid** A quadrilateral with only one pair of parallel sides.

**triangle** A polygon with 3 sides.

**underestimate** An estimate that is less than the exact answer.

**unit angle** An angle that cuts off $\frac{1}{360}$ of a circle and measures 1°.

**unit fraction** A fraction with a numerator of 1. *Example:* $\frac{1}{2}$

**unknown** A symbol or letter, such as *x*, that represents a number in an expression or equation.

**variable** A symbol or letter that stands for a number.

**vertex (plural: vertices)** The point where two rays meet to form an angle.

**volume** The number of cubic units needed to fill a solid figure.

**week** A unit of time equal to 7 days.

**weight** A measure of how heavy an object is.

**whole numbers** The numbers 0, 1, 2, 3, 4, and so on.

**yard (yd)** A customary unit of length. 1 yard = 3 feet

**year** A unit of time equal to 365 days or 52 weeks or 12 months.

**Zero Property of Multiplication** The product of any number and zero is zero. *Examples:* $3 \times 0 = 0$; $5 \times 0 = 0$

# enVision® Mathematics

## Photographs

Every effort has been made to secure permission and provide appropriate credit for photographic material. The publisher deeply regrets any omission and pledges to correct errors called to its attention in subsequent editions.

Unless otherwise acknowledged, all photographs are the property of Savvas Learning Company LLC.

Photo locators denoted as follows: Top (T), Center (C), Bottom (B), Left (L), Right (R), Background (Bkgd)

**1** MarclSchauer/Shutterstock; **3** (T) Cowardlion/Shutterstock, (C) Dabarti CGI/Shutterstock, (B) Birgit Tyrrell/Alamy Stock Photo; **4** (Bkgrd) Monkey Business Images/Shutterstock; Ajt/Shutterstock, **24** Petr84/Fotolia. **33** forkART Photography/Fotolia; **35** (T) Sean Pavone/Shutterstock, **35** (B) North Wind Picture Archives/Alamy Stock Photo; **36** (T) Naeblys/Alamy Stock Photo; **36** (B) Beata Bar/Shutterstock; **38** Richard Cavalleri/Shutterstock; **50** Alexey Usachev/Fotolia; **54** Pavel L Photo and Video/Shutterstock; **60** Digital Vision/Thinkstock; **66** WaterFrame_mus/Alamy Stock Photo. **77** John Hoffman/Shutterstock; **79** (T) Vm2002/Shutterstock, (C) DenGuy/E+/Getty Images, (B) Viju Jose/Shutterstock; **80** (Bkgrd) Ivonne Wierink/Shutterstock; AlexLMX/Shutterstock, **98** Stevanzz/Fotolia; **112** Andrew Breeden/Fotolia. **125** Majeczka/Shutterstock; **127** (T) RosalreneBetancourt 5/Alamy Stock Photo, (B) Rolf Nussbaumer Photography/Bill Draker/Rolfnp/Alamy Stock Photo; **128** (T) John Green/Cal Sport Media/Alamy Stock Photo, (B) Christophe Petit Tesson/Epa/REX/Shutterstock; **148** Steve Byland/Shutterstock; **152** 2011/Photos To Go. **165** Mark McClare/Shutterstock; **166** CristinaMuraca/Shutterstock; **167** (T) Stephen Vincent/Alamy Stock Photo, (C) Colors and shapes of underwater world/Moment/Getty Images, (B) Tierfotoagentur/A. Mirsberger/Alamy Stock Photo; **168** (Bkgrd) Konstantin Gushcha/Shutterstock, Andrey Armyagov/Shutterstock. **221** ShutterStock; **223** (T) Itsik Marom/Alamy Stock Photo, (B) David Fleetham/Alamy Stock Photo; **224** (T) Brian Lasenby/Shutterstock, (B) Willyam Bradberry/Shutterstock; **236** (L) JackF/Fotolia; (R) Smileus/Shutterstock. **257** ShutterStock; **259** (T) Danita Delimont/Alamy Stock Photo, (C) Keith Birmingham/Pasadena Star-News/San Gabriel Valley Tribune/ZUMA Wire/Alamy Live News/Alamy Stock Photo, (B) Nikola Obradovic/Shutterstock; **260** (Bkgrd) Simon Belcher/Alamy Stock Photo; Ivonne Wierink/Shutterstock, **268** Comstock Images/Jupiter Images;

**270** Womue/Fotolia. **289** Kletr/Shutterstock; **291** (T) Robert Stainforth/Alamy Stock Photo, (B) T.W. van Urk/Shutterstock; **292** (T) Oksana Mizina/Shutterstock, (B) Elnur/Shutterstock; **296** Hamik/Fotolia. **329** Adrio Communications Ltd/Shutterstock; **331** (T) Goodluz/Shutterstock, (C) Everett Collection Inc/Alamy Stock Photo, (B) Xuanhuongho/Shutterstock; **332** (Bkgrd) Rattiya Thongdumhyu/Shutterstock; AlenKadr/Shutterstock, **336** Oleksii Sagitov/Shutterstock; **364** Werner Dreblow/Fotolia. **381** Pk7comcastnet/Fotolia; **383** (T) 123RF, (B) Monkey Business Images/Shutterstock; **384** (T) Hxdyl/Shutterstock, (B) Realy Easy Star/Caterina Soprana/Alamy Stock Photo; **394** JLV Image Works/Fotolia. **413** NASA; **415** (T) Oliveromg/Shutterstock, (C) Radius Images/Alamy Stock Photo, (B) Tuasiwatn/Shutterstock; **416** (Bkgrd) Tom Wang/Shutterstock, (T) Yuliya Evstratenko/Shutterstock, (B) KK Tan/Shutterstock. **441** Bork/Shutterstock; **443** (T) Lynn Y/Shutterstock, (B) Evren Kalin Bacak/Shutterstock; **444** (T) Narin Nonthamand/Shutterstock, (B) Richard Brown/Alamy Stock Photo; **448** Hemera Technologies/ThinkStock; **461** StockPhotosArt/Fotolia; **475** (L) Proedding/Fotolia, (CL) Donfink/Fotolia (CR) Tim elliott/Fotolia, (R) Peterggyure/Fotolia; **476** Redwood/Fotolia. **477** Katrina Brown/Fotolia; **479** (T) Mark Winfrey/Shutterstock, (C) Borisov Studio/Shutterstock, (B) Fototaras/Shutterstock; **480** (Bkgrd) John Dorado/Shutterstock, (T) Poznyakov/Shutterstock, (B) Billion Photos/Shutterstock; **489** (L) Glass and Nature/Shutterstock, (C) Fesus Robert/Shutterstock, (R) Kseniya Abramova/123RF; **492** Duncan Noakes/Fotolia; **500** Sergio Martínez/Fotolia; **513** (T) Margouillat photo/Shutterstock, (B) LittleMiss/Shutterstock; **516** (T) Margouillat photo/Shutterstock, (B) Little Miss/Shutterstock. **517** luchschen/Shutterstock; **519** (T) David McGill71/Shutterstock, (B) Catarena/123RF; **520** (T) Homo Cosmicos/Shutterstock, (B) Matthew Wilkinson/Alamy Stock Photo; **524** Chinatown/Alamy Stock Photo; **526** Photo24/Stockbyte/Getty Images. **545** James Kingman/Shutterstock; **547** (T) Oleksiy Avtomonov/Shutterstock, (C) Jules_Kitano/Shutterstock, (B) Petruk Viktor/Shutterstock; **548** (Bkgrd) Peter Etchells/Shutterstock, Sarapon/Shutterstock; **579** WitR/Shutterstock. **581** Dja65/Shutterstock; **583** (T) Mukul Gupchup/Ephotocorp/Alamy Stock Photo, (B) Sean Pavone/Shutterstock; **584** (T) Mariia Tagirova/Shutterstock, (B) Edwin Godinho/Shutterstock; **586** Arina P Habich/Shutterstock; **600** Gary Blakeley/Fotolia; **616** (T) Thampapon/Shutterstock, (B) Orhan Cam/Shutterstock